Other titles by Laurie Aker and Thistlebend Ministries can be found at www.thistlebend.org.

Falling in Love Again with Your Lord
Falling in Love Again with Your Husband
Falling in Love Again with Your Children
Heart of a Woman: A Thistlebend Expository Discipleship Study
Jesus, I Need You
Jesus, I Want to Love You
Who Am I in Christ?
Beyond Belief

More than 35 electronic devotional titles by Laurie Aker and Thistlebend Ministries are also available at Bible.com and by downloading the Bible app by Life.Church and searching for plans by Thistlebend Ministries.

Thistlebend Ministries provides resources for calling, equipping, and encouraging women to know Jesus and follow Him in love and obedience. We serve churches, ministry leaders, small groups, and individuals through:

- Expository discipleship Bible studies with companion children's and family curriculum
- Devotional studies for the pursuit of spiritual growth and personal holiness
- Corresponding video and audio teaching online or on DVD
- Tools for teaching and training women how to take the truth of God's Word to heart and bring it to life
- Mentoring and discipleship training for leaders
- Full-service online resource center and support staff
- Study and training center in Louisville, KY

Please visit www.thistlebend.org for more information. Thistlebend Ministries is located in Louisville, KY.

Lord, Look Inside My Heart

Engaging in the Joy of Our Role in Sanctification

Laurie Aker

WESTBOW
PRESS®
A DIVISION OF THOMAS NELSON
& ZONDERVAN

WestBow Press books may be ordered through booksellers or by contacting:

WestBow Press
A Division of Thomas Nelson & Zondervan
1663 Liberty Drive
Bloomington, IN 47403
www.westbowpress.com
1 (866) 928-1240

ISBN: 978-1-5127-6951-7 (sc)
ISBN: 978-1-5127-6953-1 (hc)
ISBN: 978-1-5127-6952-4 (e)

Library of Congress Control Number: 2016921225

Print information available on the last page.

WestBow Press rev. date: 03/07/2017

Dedication

This book is dedicated to my husband, Kevin Aker, and to the Thistlebend Ministries Executive Vice President Hope Walrad, Ministry Assistant Kevin Purslow, and the Executive Leadership Team of Kathleen Donaldson, Susan Sampson, Amy Sizemore, and Angie Thomas. This work is the result of the prayers and devotion of these dear friends and partners in the gospel.

Epigraph

Psalm 1

1 Blessed is the man
     who walks not in the counsel of the wicked,
  nor stands in the way of sinners,
     nor sits in the seat of scoffers;
2 but his delight is in the law of the Lord,
  and on his law he meditates day and night.

3 He is like a tree
     planted by streams of water
  that yields its fruit in its season,
     and its leaf does not wither.
  In all that he does, he prospers.
4 The wicked are not so,
     but are like chaff that the wind drives away.

5 Therefore the wicked will not stand in the judgment,
     nor sinners in the congregation of the righteous;
6 for the Lord knows the way of the righteous,
     but the way of the wicked will perish.

Contents

Acknowledgement

Thank you to all the Friends of Thistlebend for their prayers, support, and generosity. A special thank you to the Kaczorowski family and the Price Foundation.

Foreword

A great Christian theologian once began his greatest work with these truths: "Without knowledge of self there is no knowledge of God," and "Without knowledge of God there is no knowledge of self." What he meant was that if we are truly to understand who *God* is as a merciful, loving, and compassionate heavenly Father, we first have to understand who *we* are as people created in His image and yet sinners before him. But in order to understand our own hearts in that way, we must look deeply into God's Word and let it expose our finitude, our sin, and our need for a Savior.

Knowledge of self, and knowledge of God.

That's what Laurie Aker and the team at Thistlebend Ministries are aiming to cultivate in this book, *Lord, Look Inside My Heart*. Full of spiritual insight and built firmly (and frequently!) on quotations from the Bible, this little book is a sweet and profound journey into knowing yourself in the light of God. It's not an easy journey—asking God to reveal your own heart to you never is—but it will be deeply rewarding! You'll not only learn about, but be equipped to practice the spiritual disciplines of prayer, repentance, fasting, and self-examination in the light of Scripture. What's more, Laurie herself is a sure and compassionate guide through this journey of Bible-based self discovery. Not only is she an able teacher of God's Word, but she has also struggled in her own life with her own sin and her struggle to know herself and her Savior. The result is a book full of heart and humor and compassionate help and encouragement. By the end of the book, I honestly think you'll feel like you know Laurie not just as an author, but as a friend!

And of course, infinitely more important than that is that I think you'll come away knowing more intimately the depth of sin in your heart—and therefore loving more intimately the One who died and rose again to save you from it!

One final note: I really cannot say enough about Laurie, her husband Kevin, and the rest of the team at Thistlebend Ministries. These are dear and serious saints who are committed not in the least to building their own kingdom or "publishing empire," but to providing resources for the use and good of the local church. As the pastor of a local church, I'm deeply familiar with the frustration of having to watch men and women under my care be swept away by books and "programs" that are selfish at best and unbiblical at worst. But I'm thrilled to say that in Thistlebend Ministries, I've found a set of resources and a group of partners who will be a great help in discipling the women who are members of my church—not a hindrance to that goal, and not in competition with it. If you're looking for discipleship tools for women that are theologically sound, biblically solid, and spiritually insightful, I don't think you'll do better than Thistlebend resources.

So off we go on this journey! Ask God to use His Word to show you yourself—and then lead you through that knowledge to know and love Jesus more.

Greg Gilbert
Pastor, Third Avenue Baptist Church
Louisville, Kentucky
2017

Introduction

by Scott Kaczorowski

Sometimes we are scared to look within. After all, we might not like what we find there. We might have the perfect picture of ourselves that we have manufactured in our mind's eye shattered by the realization that we still have weeds of sin deeply entwined in certain furrows of our heart. And then would begin the difficult task of digging down and pulling up these roots from some very delicate places. Perhaps, we may think, it is easier to be ignorant and let these things go. But if we let them go, the weeds will continue to grow, and the kind of fruit they bear will hinder our walk with the Lord. If we desire to bear the fruit of righteousness in our hearts, we must—with the Lord's help of course—explore these places, uproot these sins, and plant seeds of righteousness instead.

This book is designed to help you with this very sensitive task of tending to your heart. It will walk you through the process of beginning to open up your heart to the Lord for Him to search, care for, and tend your soul. Although heart-gardening is not always easy and relaxing, the harvest will be well worth the toil. If you are dependent on the Lord, keeping your eyes fixed on Him, and diligent in His grace, you will begin to see your heart become more and more like His. The ultimate goal of pursuing a transformed heart is that others would see Jesus and worship Him and that you would enjoy Him all the more. "I waited patiently for the LORD; he inclined to me and heard my cry. He drew me up from the pit of destruction, out of the miry bog, and set my feet upon a rock, making my steps secure. He put a new song in my mouth, a song of praise to our God. Many will see and fear, and put their trust in the LORD" (Psalm 40:1-3).

When you are finished with these pages, we hope that you will continue to use the graphics, resources, and principles presented here to continue to open up your heart to the Lord so that He may plant there a garden of His righteousness. For those who desire to dig even deeper, we highly recommend *Heart of a Woman*, the full Thistlebend Discipleship Study from which this book has been adapted. It is available at www. thistlebend.org.

CHAPTER 1

Planted by Streams of Water

As I sit high atop Signal Mountain, it is a crisp, clear, cold winter day with the brightest of bright blue skies. There is not a cloud in sight. This is my favorite sky of all. My son Noel, however, insists there must be a few clouds in the sky to break up the expanse of blue. But without a doubt, the endless blue sky is my favorite. The light is streaming in the windows, there is very little humidity in the air, and you can see forever. It is such a different day than yesterday. Yesterday was a very dark, very rainy, foggy day.

As I was heading to my daughter's home in Chattanooga, I drove up the switchback road they call "the W." I was so glad that I was nearing the end of a very long and challenging day of travel. The falling rain, combined with the amount of water spraying up from the freeway, made for poor visibility. Tired and very anxious to reach my destination, I didn't really want to stop at the grocery store, but I needed to pick up a few treats for my granddaughter. Thankfully, I found a parking spot near the door and was able to make it in without getting drenched. I tried to quickly find the items I was looking for in this unfamiliar store and get in line.

As I reached the checkout lane, the clerk asked, "How are you?" I said, "I am great, thank you. How are you?" Her head turned suddenly, and she looked at me with surprise and asked, "Really? Even when it has been such an awful, rainy day? How can you be so great on a day like today?" I said a quick, silent prayer. I responded that I had just arrived from out of town and was excited about visiting my new grandbaby and my daughter, son-in-law, and granddaughter. I asked her if she was having a difficult day. As she was giving me my receipt, she explained she was having a very difficult year and that a lot of very hard things had happened. I asked her for her name and told her that I would be praying for her. She told me her name was Penny. I was already holding up the line when I received a phone call from my daughter Hannah to see if I had already left the store. I told her I hadn't. She then asked if I would please pick up some vegetable oil. We all laughed, and I headed back to the aisles.

Searching for the Wesson gave me a few more minutes to think and to pray. I wanted to tell Penny right then that it was Jesus who gave me comfort and joy in the midst of all my circumstances, no matter the weather. I wanted to tell her that it was His presence in my life and in my heart that was giving me joy, but I hesitated because I needed to gather my thoughts. I felt that if I wasn't careful I would not be telling her the whole truth. I needed the Lord's help to share the truth and to share it in a way that would be a blessing and an encouragement to her. Yes, I needed to tell her that Jesus is the source of my joy and my strength … but I also needed to tell her that even with Jesus in my life and even as a mature Christian woman who taught Bible studies, I had known some really rough times not too long ago when I wasn't filled with joy. During that period, I had to come to grips with the fact that there was a difference between what God's Word taught me and the reality of what was truly going on in my heart and in my mind.

The Bible teaches that the joy of the Lord is to be our strength and that we are to rejoice in Him always, but I knew painfully all too well that I hadn't trusted in the joy of the Lord to be my strength in those very difficult times. It had been a jolting, disturbing realization. I had been through many trials before and found myself able to walk forward in joy and know His comfort, but that had not been the case in this most recent trial. At the time, I was reeling from the shock of my response. The words of Psalm 1 also came to mind, "Blessed is the man who walks not in the counsel of the wicked, nor stands in the way of sinners, nor sits in the seat of scoffers; but his delight is in the law of the LORD, and on his law he meditates day and night. He is like a tree planted by streams of water that yields its fruit in its season, and its leaf does not wither. In all that he does, he prospers." I desperately longed to be like a tree firmly planted by streams of water, bearing fruit in season, whose leaves did not wither. But that just wasn't the case. I was forced to reexamine my heart, my thoughts, my priorities, and my affections. What was it that I held so dear? I thought I knew my Savior's love for me. I thought He was my all in all. But I was finding out He wasn't. We think we understand the affections of our hearts, but only One knows. My life was flashing before me. I was straining to see what I was truly standing upon. What was I holding near and dear in my heart? Where did I place my trust? I discovered there were things hidden in my heart—fear, doubt, and hurt—all of which I had been unaware. And, oh, what pain they caused.

So I needed to think through how I might share all of this with Penny, the cashier at Pruett's. As I found the vegetable oil and made my way back to her register, I determined that I would pray and seek the Lord about how to reach out to her in the most effective way. As I paid for my item, I shared with Penny that I had been through some pretty tough times recently as well, and I told her that I would be praying for her. I made a plan to be back in touch with Penny before I left Signal Mountain.

If we are in Christ, our hearts have been forever changed. We have been given new hearts that have the ability to know joy even in the most difficult circumstances. We have been given the desire for righteousness, holiness, and truth. We have been rescued and cleansed, and we have had our sin paid for in full by the blood of Christ! Not only has the penalty of our sin been paid for, but we have also been given the power to overcome sin and the hope of living in heaven one day without the presence of sin.

We also have been given the Holy Spirit—God himself—and His inheritance! And as if that weren't enough, we have been given access to the throne room of God, always and forever, to ask for and bring before Him anything and everything. "How unsearchable are his judgments and how inscrutable his ways" (Romans 11:33). We want to do everything we can then to embrace our new inheritance!

In his first epistle, the apostle Peter exhorts all of us who know God and who are called by Him to get our priorities right, to prepare our minds for action, and to set our hope on Jesus (1 Peter 1:13). He teaches us that since we have been redeemed, rescued, and given a new hope, we need to get ready to serve the Lord and to focus! "Therefore, preparing your minds for action, and being sober-minded, set your hope fully on the grace that will be brought to you at the revelation of Jesus Christ.

As obedient children, do not be conformed to the passions of your former ignorance, but as he who called you is holy, you also be holy in all your conduct, since it is written, 'You shall be holy, for I am holy'" (1 Peter 1:13-16). This is what Peter says we should strive for, yet most of us find ourselves running after worthless things, bound by our human emotions, tainted by sin, and steeped in worrying, fretting, and craving. We are human vessels made of flesh; we are jars of clay! Oh, yes, we have been redeemed, bought by the blood of Christ, but we must overcome our wily flesh that has been invaded by sin! We can only do this through the power of the Holy Spirit. And I say "wily" because my flesh is wily, but some of you maybe are not so wily as you are asleep, sun bathing, or being Miss Molly-Do-Right!

We have been commanded to join in the work of overcoming our remaining sin, trusting in the power we have been given in the Holy Spirit and in the grace and forgiveness we have been given in Christ—for we are not able to do it alone. This work will be a battle, though. "For the desires of the flesh are against the spirit, and the desires of the spirit are against the flesh" (Galatians 5:17). In every believer's heart there is a constant struggle between the old man and the new, and we can be blind sometimes to the old man who creeps back in or that never really was put to death. Listen to John Owen's perspective:

> Sin sets its strength against every act of holiness, and against every degree we grow to. Let not that woman* think she makes any progress in holiness who walks not over the bellies of her lusts. She who does not kill sin in her way takes no steps towards her journey's end. She who finds not opposition from it, and who sets not herself in every particular to its mortification, is at peace with it, not dying to it.[1]

We need to ask God to give us eyes to see our sinful ways so that we are able to get to the root of them and so that we can recognize our sin and overcome it. Paul says in Ephesians 4:21-24, "you have heard about him and were taught in him, as the truth is in Jesus, to put off your old self, which belongs to your former manner of life and is corrupt through deceitful desires, and to be renewed in the spirit of your minds, and to put on the new self, created after the likeness of God in true righteousness and holiness." We want to turn toward God, draw near to Him, and have Him search our hearts.

We want to be rooted and established in Christ, filled with Christ, and overflowing with Christ—and not ourselves! If we want to walk in the Spirit and not live out the desires of the flesh, we have work to do: "Therefore, my beloved, as you have always obeyed, so now, not only as in my presence but much more in my absence, work out your own salvation with fear and trembling, for it is God who works in you, both to will and to work for his good pleasure" (Philippians 2:12-13). We must be about the work the Lord has called us to do, the work of walking out our salvation.

Paul further says that since we have put off the old woman we are to now put away our old ways: "Therefore, having put away falsehood, let each one of you speak the truth with his neighbor, for we are members one of another. Be angry and do not sin; do not let the sun go down on your anger, and give no opportunity to the devil. Let the thief no longer steal, but rather let him labor, doing honest work with his own hands, so that he may have something to share with anyone in need" (Ephesians 4:25-28).

As with a garden, if we don't dig up the roots of these weeds in our hearts, they will overtake our hearts and choke the life right out of us! The fleshly roots of our hearts wrap themselves around and cling to the most insidious, distasteful, and worthless things, making way for the weeds of sin to sprout in our hearts. However, if we instead dig up the weeds, all the way down to the roots that are wrapped around our sins, and separate them from the roots of righteousness in our hearts placed there by Christ, we enable the good roots to penetrate deep into the rich soil—into Christ—into the river of living water. A color-filled, fragrant, and abundant life will begin to blossom. We will be rooted and established in love himself.

5

So, by grace through faith we are going to ask the Lord to search our hearts and help us get to the root of our sin by allowing Him to reveal to us what lies deep in our hearts. In 2 Corinthians 13:5 Paul says, "Examine yourselves, to see whether you are in the faith. Test yourselves. Or do you not realize this about yourselves, that Jesus Christ is in you?—unless indeed you fail to meet the test!" And then, by His grace, as we pick up our cross, die to self, and confess and repent of our sins, a powerful, life-changing work will be accomplished in us. We will be impacting generations.

Getting to the root of our sins is a process, a life-long process. When we are in Christ, the Father sees us through Him. We are precious in His sight, and He adores us with a love we have a hard time comprehending. But this week, and in the weeks to follow, will you make it your goal to choose to believe that He loves you, right where you are—imperfect, sinful, and distinctly His? He loves you, not because of your performance, but because of your position in Christ. Be patient and allow Him to lead and do His work, His way.

There are times when the Lord will deliver us from strongholds of sin immediately. However, much of the time, God works slowly and deliberately. His desire is to have a close, intimate relationship with us, and he achieves this by making us dependent upon Him. He is looking for your trust and obedience, not your perfection. His Son is perfect and has already fulfilled all of the requirements of the law for you. Together with the Lord, you are working out your salvation. Christ is your righteousness and is working in and through you. It is all part of His wise and more than wonderful plan. He is building a new kingdom in your heart, not unlike when He built the new temple through Solomon! Breaking down the old and replacing it with the new is only possible through the mercy, power, and grace of God! It involves crying out to the Lord and listening to Him. We want to learn to ask God for all we need. Look to Him and plead. Listen to King Solomon's request in the face of a huge task and hear God's response. Take it to heart:

> Solomon loved the LORD, walking in the statutes of David his father ... At Gibeon the LORD appeared to Solomon in a dream by night, and God said, "Ask what I shall give

you." And Solomon said, "You have shown great and steadfast love to your servant David my father, because he walked before you in faithfulness, in righteousness, and in uprightness of heart toward you. And you have kept for him this great and steadfast love and have given him a son to sit on his throne this day. And now, O Lord my God, you have made your servant king in place of David my father, although I am but a little child. I do not know how to go out or come in. And your servant is in the midst of your people whom you have chosen, a great people, too many to be numbered or counted for multitude. Give your servant therefore an understanding mind to govern your people, that I may discern between good and evil, for who is able to govern this your great people?" It pleased the Lord that Solomon had asked this. And God said to him, "Because you have asked this, and have not asked for yourself long life or riches or the life of your enemies, but have asked for yourself understanding[2] to discern what is right, behold, I now do according to your word. Behold, I give you a wise and discerning mind, so that none like you has been before you and none like you shall arise after you. I give you also what you have not asked, both riches and honor, so that no other king shall compare with you, all your days. And if you will walk in my ways, keeping my statutes and my commandments, as your father David walked, then I will lengthen your days." (1 Kings 3:3-14)

Choose to partner with your Lord and ask Him to give you wisdom as He gave it to Solomon. As you begin this process and as the Lord reveals your sin, you may feel more than a little overwhelmed by the sense of your unholiness. Do not be discouraged; although it may feel awful, it is a good thing. It is a wonderful and beautiful work you are doing and one that will impact generations to come.

Each time you see your sin, remember to look to Jesus, your Savior and your Lord, and hide yourself in Him. And remember, there is now "no condemnation for those who are in Christ Jesus" (Romans 8:1). When you feel particularly discouraged and want to give up, run into the arms of your Savior and Lord. "The name of the Lord is a strong tower; the righteous runs into it and is safe" (Proverbs 18:10). Practice fixing your eyes upon Him and putting your trust in Him and in His mercy and grace. He loves you and loved you while you were yet a sinner. If you have surrendered your life to Him, it is very important to remember your position in Him. You are no longer who you once were; you now are in Christ and want to walk forward in Him. This endeavor is well worth your effort, because a great harvest lies ahead.

Interacting with God and His Word

At the end of each chapter you will be offered a time to interact with God and His Word in an intimate and personal way through the psalms. You may write your thoughts or answers in a prayer journal or in the space provided at the end of each chapter.

It is so helpful to carefully observe the psalms of David because of his relationship with God and his pursuit of righteousness. We can learn from David and observe how he approaches God in prayer. We can also learn much about how to have an intimate and real relationship with the Lord as we observe David's understanding of God and his response to God and His Word.

For years I longed for a mentor, someone who would teach me how to walk with God and have an intimate relationship with Him. Surprisingly, the Lord didn't bring a living person into my life, but led me to sit under David, a man who lived thousands of years ago! It was in his psalms that I learned so much about God and about how my heart should respond to Him. I am praying and trusting that God will do the same for you as you seek after Him with all your heart. Ask the Lord to grant you His grace to walk forward in faith to overcome sin and receive the joy of your salvation!

Let's begin by reading Psalm 1.

Psalm 1

1   Blessed is the man
        who walks not in the counsel of the wicked,

nor stands in the way of sinners,
    nor sits in the seat of scoffers;
2 but his delight is in the law of the LORD,
    and on his law he meditates day and night.

3 He is like a tree
    planted by streams of water
that yields its fruit in its season,
    and its leaf does not wither.
In all that he does, he prospers.
4 The wicked are not so,
    but are like chaff that the wind drives away.

5 Therefore the wicked will not stand in the judgment,
    nor sinners in the congregation of the righteous;
6 for the LORD knows the way of the righteous,
    but the way of the wicked will perish.

Read verses 1-3 a second time. What does this passage say the blessed man does *not* do? What does he *do*? What are the results of his choices? Now ask yourself, "Is your delight in the law of the Lord?" Instead, do you find yourself delighting in many worldly things? If so, ask the Lord to help you see and confess where your desires are not pleasing to Him or where your priorities may be off. As you close this section, ask the Lord to help you be like the tree planted by streams of water, bearing its fruit in season.

Search My Heart, O God

Also at the end of each chapter, we will read and pray through excerpts from Psalm 139 and ask the Lord to search our hearts and help form, shape, and direct our hearts to be like His. Again, feel free to write your thoughts or answers to any questions in this section in a prayer journal or in the space provided at the end of each chapter.

This first time, read and pray through all of Psalm 139. As you read, highlight or underline the words of encouragement. Speak these truths to your heart.

Psalm 139

1 O Lord, you have searched me and known me!
2 You know when I sit down and when I rise up;
      you discern my thoughts from afar.
3 You search out my path and my lying down
      and are acquainted with all my ways.
4 Even before a word is on my tongue,
      behold, O Lord, you know it altogether.
5 You hem me in, behind and before,
      and lay your hand upon me.
6 Such knowledge is too wonderful for me;
      it is high; I cannot attain it.

7 Where shall I go from your Spirit?
      Or where shall I flee from your presence?
8 If I ascend to heaven, you are there!
      If I make my bed in Sheol, you are there!
9 If I take the wings of the morning
      and dwell in the uttermost parts of the sea,
10 even there your hand shall lead me,
      and your right hand shall hold me.
11 If I say, "Surely the darkness shall cover me,
      and the light about me be night,"
12 even the darkness is not dark to you;
      the night is bright as the day,
      for darkness is as light with you.

13 For you formed my inward parts;
      you knitted me together in my mother's womb.
14 I praise you, for I am fearfully and wonderfully made.
    Wonderful are your works;
      my soul knows it very well.
15 My frame was not hidden from you,
    when I was being made in secret,
      intricately woven in the depths of the earth.

16 Your eyes saw my unformed substance;
    in your book were written, every one of them,
      the days that were formed for me,
      when as yet there was none of them.

17 How precious to me are your thoughts, O God!
    How vast is the sum of them!
18 If I would count them, they are more than the sand.
    I awake, and I am still with you.

19 Oh that you would slay the wicked, O God!
    O men of blood, depart from me!
20 They speak against you with malicious intent;
    your enemies take your name in vain.
21 Do I not hate those who hate you, O Lord?
    And do I not loathe those who rise up against you?
22 I hate them with complete hatred;
    I count them my enemies.

23 Search me, O God, and know my heart!
    Try me and know my thoughts!
24 And see if there be any grievous way in me,
    and lead me in the way everlasting!

David, who was once a shepherd boy and then anointed king by God, is described in the Bible as a man after God's heart. Notice that he is asking God to search his heart. David asks the Lord to go deep. And he not only asks Him to search his heart, but he bravely also asks God to try him! He is asking the Lord to bring trials and tests into his life to reveal the reality of his heart. This is not our earthly mind-set. David was well acquainted with trials and yet he asked for more. He desired to have a heart like God's.

We so desperately hope the Lord won't bring trials into our lives and often feel that if He really loved us He would protect us from them. Yet our faith is forged through them!

So we are going to do something different! At the end of each chapter, we are going to read from Psalm 139 as mentioned and then make the last two verses of this Psalm the cry of our hearts.

Not only does the Lord refine and strengthen our faith through trials, but, as we will learn so clearly in this book, the Lord brings the hidden things of our hearts to light through trials—not only the good and the bad, but also the most praiseworthy! Listen to 1 Peter 1:6-7: "In this you rejoice, though now for a little while, if necessary, you have been grieved by various trials, so that the tested genuineness of your faith—more precious than gold that perishes though it is tested by fire—may be found to result in praise and glory and honor at the revelation of Jesus Christ." Trials are a powerful tool of the Lord.

Ask the Lord to test and try you to reveal any unrighteousness in your heart. "Search me, O God, and know my heart! Try me and know my thoughts! And see if there be any grievous way in me, and lead me in the way everlasting!"

Ask the Lord to bring your actions, your words, your thinking, and your feelings to your attention. Don't be afraid. As He reveals to you your ways, ask Him to teach you His ways. When necessary confess your sin and ask God for the grace to turn from your sin and walk forward in His righteousness.

This devotional has been written to those who have believed in the Lord Jesus Christ and trusted in Him to deal with their sin. It is only through Christ and by His grace that our hearts can be transformed. If this is new to you or you are uncertain of your position with God, I encourage you to take a moment now to read "The Gospel of Our Salvation" in the Appendix.

Close in ACTS Prayer

Adoration - Praise God for Who He Is

Confession - Admit Your Sins with a Repentant Heart

Thanksgiving - Thank God for All He Has Done, Is Doing, and Is Going to Do

Supplication - Make Your Requests to God for Yourself and On Behalf of Others.

Here is an example of this type of prayer for you to follow:

Adoration: O Lord God Almighty, I praise you for who you are! You are the creator of the heavens and earth, all that I can see and all that I can't see. You sustain all life and hold the planets in their place. You rule and reign at all times over all things. You alone are worthy of all my worship!

Confession: O Father, I love you, and I want to honor you in all I do and say. I confess that my words are often harsh and unkind with my children. I am afraid of losing control and like to keep things manageable. But when life with them gets chaotic, I easily snap. Please forgive my actions and my fear and give me love and compassion for them. Help work repentance in me and help me trust in Christ my Savior and His power.

Thanksgiving: Heavenly Father, I thank you for your loving-kindness and compassion to me. Help me be forever thankful for all you do to make me more like your Son and all you do to watch over and provide for me each day. I will be thankful and trust you in all things.

Supplication: Abba, Father, you are my all in all. You are my everything. I trust you with all my weaknesses, needs, hurts, and concerns. I come to you to intercede on behalf of those in my life and others you have called me to pray for. I pray for …

Notes

CHAPTER 2

Preparing to Ask God to Search Your Heart

It can be frightening to look within. If the thought of digging down below the surface makes you feel unsure and apprehensive, please don't walk away or unconsciously lay this book aside. It may feel very uncomfortable to step into the internal, but doing so will bring about the greatest joy, freedom, and hope you have ever known. You will come to know the love, the compassion, the power, and the mercy of Jesus in a way you may never have known. He longs for us to come to Him. Our tender shepherd stands, holding His arms out for us. He beckons us to come; He entreats us to be reconciled. Listen to the Scripture in John 7:37: "Jesus stood up and cried out, 'If anyone thirsts, let him come to me and drink.'"

We run, we hide, we cover up, we keep busy, we clean, we go shopping, we volunteer, we do anything we can to keep from being alone with ourselves and allowing God to search our hearts and find the darkness that exists there. There are things we know God wants to address in our lives, but we resist. We don't want to deal with the unlovely, the uncomfortable, or the unknown. Interestingly enough, the Lord already knows all that is there. He knows exactly what it is, and He has provided all we need to remove it. Yet, we resist.

True freedom, peace, and joy are right around the corner, available to us freely from Christ, but we settle for a mere simulacrum, which initially satisfies our flesh, curbs our appetite for the true food, but really never fully satisfies. We are left empty and craving more of whatever we are searching for. We often just want to have our needs met, and, the truth be known, we just really want things to be enjoyable and comfortable. And instead it appears as though Jesus is calling us to this drab, stark existence, a walk of death and dying.

We look around at the people who seem to have surrendered their lives to Him; we see all of the trouble and difficulties they face, and we want to quickly walk the other way. Whether we are Christians or not, the enemy of Christ, the devil, does all that he can to dissuade us from seeking righteousness, trying to make it seem even more difficult than it really is, because he knows full well that it is the path to life and abundance. The more we resist and push away the thoughts of our sin and our failures, the more guilty we feel—and often so guilty that we don't even want to face our Savior, our Lord Jesus Christ! This is exactly what Satan (the enemy) desires.

We want to draw near to God and ask Him to peer deeply into the depths of our hearts. Trust His love and His gentleness. As you sit by yourself, in the quiet of your home, with no one around, faithfully and humbly approach your Lord, your shepherd, and ask Him why you resist. Please don't be afraid. Listen to the Scripture: "Perfect love casts out all fear" (1 John 4:18). You may not love the Lord perfectly, but when you are in Christ, He loves you perfectly! He has already demonstrated His love for you: "God shows his love for us in that while we were still sinners, Christ died for us" (Romans 5:8).

As you begin to ask God to search your innermost being, do not be frightened. You may very likely begin to feel discouraged or overwhelmed. This certainly would be normal, but it's not the intent or the purpose. Remember, He has gone before you long ago and provided for you in His Son, your Savior. Allow your gentle, tender, loving shepherd to probe into the darkness of your soul with His eternal light. Keep Paul's words in mind: "There is therefore now no condemnation for those who are in

Christ Jesus" (Romans 8:1). You are in Christ. Your standing in relation to Christ makes all the difference. Hide yourself in Him and in what He has done for you. Preach the good news of the gospel to yourself each and every day. Take a minute to pause and pray right now. Ask the Lord to take you by the hand and gently walk you through the following thoughts about why we resist looking at our hearts:

Blindness. We are most often unaware of our sin. Of course there are many symptoms of our sin that we may see, but we don't really see the root of the symptoms that needs to be changed. Our remaining sin is so much a part of us. We are so familiar with the sin and it is so much a part of who we are that we don't even recognize it. We are basically blind to our sin or to strongholds in our life.

However, we often are not totally without sight. We have enough awareness of our guilt that we hide, hide, hide and cover, cover, cover! But we see things from man's perspective—the surface symptoms and the justification for them. We cannot see our sin as God sees our sin. We desperately need Him to open the eyes of our hearts because we are blind to the truth and blind to our sin. The gospel of John talks about the darkness and the light. John describes how the darkness hates the light and our fallen humanity avoids the light: "The Light shines in the darkness, and the darkness did not comprehend it" (John 1:5).

I think of my previous sin of covetousness and materialism. It had such a strong hold on me as a young Christian. I was desperate for the things of this world that would give me worth, meaning, and pleasure. I knew the Word of God. I had memorized the verses with my children in elementary school, but I did not hear them. I did not comprehend them.

The Word clearly addresses covetousness and materialism. Matthew 6:19-20 says, "Lay not up for yourselves treasures upon earth, where moth and rust doth corrupt, and where thieves break through and steal. But lay up for yourselves treasures in heaven, where neither moth nor rust doth corrupt, and where thieves do not break through nor steal." My sin was such a part of me that I had a very hard time really hearing God's Word or recognizing that it was speaking to me.

I felt so inadequate and worthless inside that I looked for anything that would give me worth. I sought significance in a world that was absorbed with self. If I had taken God at His word and seen my sin for what it was, I could have confessed my sin, repented, and been cleansed from unrighteousness. I could have been free! But I did not want to see my sin—nor see it as sin. I just looked for ways to ease my pain … buy more stuff!

Fear. It is insidious. It is as quiet as a stealth bomber and as treacherous. Fear is deceitful. It is our enemy, yet we see it as a protector, as an advisor. Fear also entraps us because we don't like change and we don't like the unknown. Besides, we are accustomed to our ways … Hey, it's the way we've always done it! We would rather live with what we already are because it is familiar. We are afraid that if we start tearing down strongholds, we will be diminished, condemned, rejected, shamed or even destroyed. The Lord already knows this fear is there. He tells us so often in the Bible to not fear: "Do not be afraid any longer, only believe" (Mark 5:36). He wants us to trust Him by looking inside to see what is really in our hearts, to confess what He shows us, and to give it all to Him. He is standing with forgiveness in His arms, yet we hide in fear.

Pride. Pride says, "I am fine the way I am. I am in control. My will first. My way." God says, "I AM." He is God; we are not. His ways are higher than our ways and He rules and reigns. "His dominion is an everlasting dominion, and his kingdom endures from generation to generation; all the inhabitants of the earth are accounted as nothing, and he does according to his will among the host of heaven and among the inhabitants of the earth; and none can stay his hand or say to him, 'What have you done?'" (Daniel 4:34-35). While God is in control, He also desires what is very best for us. He longs for us to allow Him to bless us. Oftentimes the more mature we become in our Christian walk, the more we can be inclined to think, "I've got this. I know what the Bible says … I'm doing it." But we really don't. We lack humility (or perhaps it's false humility). We fail to keep observing our actions and asking God to search our hearts, as though Christ has finished his work in us. The truth is that He never will until we are in heaven with Him. The real issue is that we really don't want to do the hard work. As long as we can keep things together on the outside and no one knows, we would rather continue on without having to deal with the unknown, with major sacrifice, or with life change. But holiness is a lifelong pursuit. 1 Peter 5:6-7 says, "Humble yourselves, therefore, under the mighty hand of God so that at the proper time he may exalt you, casting all your anxieties on him, because he cares for you." The really sad part is that we totally resist this and yet the Lord promises blessing. It is not our nature to humble ourselves under anyone!

Laziness. Pursuing holiness takes discipline, focus, and effort. It takes work, it takes time, it takes a strategy, and it takes follow through to turn from going one way to turning to another—even in doing our quiet time. Are you willing to do the work that is required? Do you believe the Lord will grant you all you need to walk in His path?

Selfishness. The big questions we have to ask ourselves are, "Whom do I care about? Who really matters? What do I say by my actions? Whom do I serve each day?" Selfishness is one of the greatest sins of mankind and of our current culture. It is particularly challenging because our culture affirms it. And let's be honest; we like our sin. It works for us. Sin does pay. We may be charged a huge interest, we may be bound and gagged by it, we may lose much of our freedom and joy, but ... we don't seem to mind.

Control. Need I say more? We don't want to lose control of our lives. God might ask us to go to Africa and wear sandals and eat bugs. The Lord calls us into a life of ongoing confession and repentance. But there needs to be a Romans 12:1 moment—or two ("present your bodies as a living sacrifice"). Sometimes we realize we need to step it up, recommit, and adjust.

Unbelief. We fail to believe that God can really do anything about our sin. We may have confessed it over and over, but nothing has happened, so we think that nothing can happen. We doubt the power of God. We may not realize that we doubt, but we do. I John 1:9 says, "If we confess our sins, he is faithful and just and will forgive us our sins and purify us from all unrighteousness." We are so acutely aware of how integrated and central our sin is to our life that we can't believe God can possibly change us. We think our sin is just part of who we are and that we will always be that way. We have been this way for so many years that we doubt God's power to transform. So we continue in our ways, believing we are unable to change, when ironically, the only reason we are unable to change, is unbelief.

How do we move from resistance to repentance? Our first step is to go before the throne of our merciful and loving Savior and confess our sins of blindness, fear, pride, laziness, selfishness, desire for control, unbelief, and any other strongholds.

Before you take time in prayer and confession ask yourself, "Am I willing to follow the Lord wherever He leads me because He is my Lord?" "Do I trust Him, His love, His wisdom, and His leading?"

Intcracting with God and His Word

Read and pray through Psalm 51.

Psalm 51

1 Have mercy on me, O God,
    according to your steadfast love;
   according to your abundant mercy
    blot out my transgressions.
2 Wash me thoroughly from my iniquity,
    and cleanse me from my sin!

3 For I know my transgressions,
    and my sin is ever before me.
4 Against you, you only, have I sinned
    and done what is evil in your sight,
   so that you may be justified in your words
    and blameless in your judgment.
5 Behold, I was brought forth in iniquity,
    and in sin did my mother conceive me.
6 Behold, you delight in truth in the inward being,
    and you teach me wisdom in the secret heart.

7 Purge me with hyssop, and I shall be clean;
    wash me, and I shall be whiter than snow.
8 Let me hear joy and gladness;
    let the bones that you have broken rejoice.
9 Hide your face from my sins,
    and blot out all my iniquities.
10 Create in me a clean heart, O God,
    and renew a right spirit within me.

11 Cast me not away from your presence,
   and take not your Holy Spirit from me.
12 Restore to me the joy of your salvation,
   and uphold me with a willing spirit.

13 Then I will teach transgressors your ways,
   and sinners will return to you.
14 Deliver me from bloodguiltiness, O God,
   O God of my salvation,
   and my tongue will sing aloud of your righteousness.
15 O Lord, open my lips,
   and my mouth will declare your praise.
16 For you will not delight in sacrifice, or I would give it;
   you will not be pleased with a burnt offering.
17 The sacrifices of God are a broken spirit;
   a broken and contrite heart, O God, you will not despise.

18 Do good to Zion in your good pleasure;
   build up the walls of Jerusalem;
19 then will you delight in right sacrifices,
   in burnt offerings and whole burnt offerings;
   then bulls will be offered on your altar.

David knows God's mercy and approaches Him with that in mind. Just when you are feeling inclined to run and hide, stop yourself and remember His deep and compassionate love for you. He loves you right where you are. He isn't looking for perfection. He is looking for you, His child, to come to Him, to bury your face in His chest, and to vulnerably abandon yourself into His hands. Remember, "There is therefore now no condemnation for those who are in Christ Jesus" (Romans 8:1). Meditate on these beautiful words. Continue to recite these words in your heart and in your mind. When you are in Christ, you have been set free from the penalty of sin! Christ was condemned in your place. You are free from oppression of the law because Jesus fulfilled it all for us. As you walk forward, you must remember to trust in His grace and His power to obey the Word through the Spirit that dwells within us. God knows full well that we are not able to keep that law perfectly; only Christ could keep

it perfectly. Knowing that you are not condemned but rather forgiven, approach God asking Him for His mercy as you confess.
Confess:

- Your blindness
- Your fear
- Your pride
- Your laziness
- Your selfishness
- Your desire for control
- Your unbelief

Search My Heart, O God

Prayerfully read the following excerpts from Psalm 139. Just as David asks God to search His heart, ask God to search yours.

Psalm 139

1 O LORD, you have searched me and known me!
2 You know when I sit down and when I rise up;
        you discern my thoughts from afar.
3 You search out my path and my lying down
        and are acquainted with all my ways.
4 Even before a word is on my tongue,
        behold, O LORD, you know it altogether.
5 You hem me in, behind and before,
        and lay your hand upon me.
6 Such knowledge is too wonderful for me;
        it is high; I cannot attain it.

23 Search me, O God, and know my heart!
        Try me and know my thoughts!
24 And see if there be any grievous way in me,
        and lead me in the way everlasting!

Is there any area in your life where you feel failure, hopelessness, or condemnation? Are you discouraged or overwhelmed? Perhaps you are feeling apathetic and don't really care whether you are more holy or pleasing to God. Tell God whatever it is you are feeling. Trust Him with it all!

Close in ACTS Prayer

Adoration - Praise God for Who He Is

Confession - Admit Your Sins with a Repentant Heart

Thanksgiving - Thank God for All He Has Done, Is Doing, and Is Going to Do

Supplication - Make Your Requests to God for Yourself and On Behalf of Others.

Notes

CHAPTER 3

I Bow My Knees Before the Father

Prayer is the open door into the private chambers of your heavenly Father. If we have any need, we can run directly, unannounced, to the God of the universe. When we are in Christ, the moment we bow our head, bend our knees, utter a cry, or even groan within our spirit, He hears us and we are in His presence. In Christ we have been given direct access to God on High. Although He is Lord of Lords, He intensely desires oneness with you, an intimate, heartbeat-by-heartbeat relationship with you. No thought, no decision, no concern is too small. When your heart is racing with excitement, paralyzed in fear, or sluggish in despair, not only does He know, He also wants you to know He knows. He wants to carry every burden. So deep is our need, so heavy our burden, but so vast is His love and grace. Until we are in heaven, we must not cease to pray.

Remember, at one time you were separated from Christ, alienated from God, a stranger to the covenants of promise, having no hope, and being without God in the world. But now in Christ, you, who once were far off, have been brought near by the blood of Christ (Ephesians 2:12-13). You can come boldly before the throne of God, in Him and because of Him. Is there anything you need? Anything? There is nothing of any value that you are able to obtain without Him, and there is nothing you need that He will not provide. Do you sense your poverty? Your sinfulness? Your inadequacy? Cry out to Him that He may show you His mercy. Do you *not* sense your poverty, sinfulness, and inadequacy? Then cry out to Him that He might show you the truth of your misery, that He then may show you His mercy! "For we do not have a high priest who is unable to sympathize with our weaknesses, but one who in every respect has been tempted as we are, yet without sin. Let us then with confidence draw near to the throne of grace, that we may receive mercy and find grace to help in time of need" (Hebrews 4:15-16).

How do we develop such a relationship? A relationship of utter dependence and oneness with Christ? We do it by spending time alone with Him, daily. We must leave this temporal world, this world of man, this world of sin, to sit at our Savior's feet and lean our head upon His chest. We must leave it continually, through prayer. As we find a quiet, lonely place and bow our hearts before Him, we enter into another world, another dimension, into heaven itself. We find ourselves at God's banquet table, in the chambers of His love and grace. We hear the voice of the psalmist as he beckons us, "Enter his gates with thanksgiving, and his courts with praise!" (Psalm 100:4). It is through humble adoration, confession, and thanksgiving that we draw near to God. We have been given this freedom to enter the holy place through Christ's shed blood. Let us not tarry, but rather let us draw near daily, often, and continually.

Draw near in humble **adoration**, praising Him with His Word, through the psalms, recounting His mighty deeds, and declaring His marvelous character, His perfect holiness, His sovereignty, and every aspect of who He is. It is through praise and adoration that we lose ourselves into the presence of God Almighty. Our eyes are lifted off of self, our mind is focused upon our Maker, and our cares and our burdens are diminished in the light of His presence. Our knowledge of Him grows, our vision is corrected, our thinking is transformed, and our faith is nurtured. God is near; God is with us.

Draw near in contrite **confession**. Hiding our sin from God is fruitless, futile, and foolish. He already knows our sin and our condition: broken, weak, bruised, abused. He alone is our Messiah, and He alone can rescue us. Let us draw near to Him with open hearts and allow Him in that He may heal us.

Thousands of years ago, David the psalmist, said, "For when I kept silent, my bones wasted away through my groaning all day long … Therefore let everyone who is godly offer prayer to you at a time when you may be found; surely in the rush of great waters, they shall not reach him. You are a hiding place for me; you preserve me from trouble; you surround me with shouts of deliverance" (Psalm 32:3, 6-7). Where did David run? Where did he hide? Let us draw near to God with all of our secrets, all of our weaknesses, and all of our sins, our regrets, and our failings. As we do, we will see the mercy and power of God, because it is only through His blood that our sins can be washed away—completely forgiven. When we humble ourselves and admit to God what He already knows about us, and when we draw near to God in faith and confess our sins, He is able to forgive us of our sins. We are not only forgiven, we are released from bondage, healed from pain, and old thinking is replaced with godly ways of thinking. We are transformed! We are more like our Lord!

Confession is an amazing and abundant provision from the Lord. He has provided a way for us, a way where there would be no way. We are so often afraid to admit our sinful ways even when our Lord stands right before us with the cure. God's abundant blessings are available to us and freedom and joy are right around the corner, but we are reluctant. We are deceived. We have tasted the way of sin and it satisfies. Our flesh is indulged, and we remain in control, or so it seems. Let us choose to remember David's testimony, "For when I kept silent, my bones wasted away through my groaning all day long." Let us go to the one who can cleanse us from all sin. May there be less of us and more of Him!

Draw near in grateful **thanksgiving**. Oh, the difference between a sour spirit and a grateful heart. Paul commands us to be thankful in everything because it affects everything. The attitude of our hearts completely determines our view. One of the greatest hindrances to a heart of thankfulness is our sense of failure or inadequacy. We often focus on trying to get it "right" rather than understanding that we never will. We often feel that we fall so far short of the mark. We see our sin ever before us and in our desire to please the Lord with our performance, we get caught in discouragement and hopelessness.

We cannot pay our debt of sin, nor atone for our sin or make everything all right. Only Christ can do these things. We are to put our trust in Christ alone. We are not to try to do what Jesus has done for us in His active obedience. He alone was able to keep the Law and fulfill all righteousness. I know from my own experience that I have felt such dismay over my sinfulness and my failures that I could see nothing else. There was a mountain looming that continued to gain in height. Our eyes can become so locked upon our sins, our inadequacies, and our failures that we see nothing else. Of course there are those that are so locked on the sins, inadequacies, and failures of others that they see nothing else.

Either way, comparing ourselves to the "perfect" specimens at church, in our neighborhood, or at work will bar us from all joy and thankfulness. Examples are often thrust before us of what the perfect Christian looks like and what they are able to do. Although it may be well intended, it can have a very adverse effect. Unfortunately, although it may appear otherwise, none of us is perfect, not even close to perfect. Christ alone is the spotless lamb. Humbling as this statement is, the fact is certain that we are all more or less suffering under the disease of sin. We continue to walk by faith, not trusting in our ability to do anything good or worthy of God's salvation, putting all of our trust in Jesus' sinless life, substitutionary death, and victorious resurrection. In Philippians 4:4, Paul exhorts us to rejoice in the Lord, and he repeats himself, "Again, I say rejoice!" He urges us further in 1 Thessalonians to rejoice always and to be thankful in all things (5:16, 18). James tells us to count it pure joy when we encounter trials (James 1:2). We must fix our eyes upon Jesus, the author and perfector of our faith, not on ourselves and our failures.

We want to cling to thankfulness in all things. We want to examine Him and His perfection, gaze upon His face and its glory, and meditate upon Him and His holiness. We must take our eyes off of ourselves long enough to see Him so that we may know Him in order to reflect Him. He is our righteousness. We are nothing apart from Him, and neither is anyone else. Let us humble ourselves before Him, fix our eyes upon Him, and be thankful—thankful for the gift of salvation, thankful for this day which He made, thankful in our circumstances, knowing He is the Lord of them, and thankful in our weakness because He is strong. Let's be thankful! Let us draw near to Him and gaze in His beautiful face!

Prayer is the open door into the private chambers of our heavenly Father. It is the true passageway to intimate communion with Christ.

Not only are we to praise Him, confess our sins to Him, and thank Him, we must *listen* to Him. The Bible is clear, "The sheep hear his voice, and he calls his own sheep by name and leads them out" (John 10:3). Prayer is about relationship with the one true God. Prayer, real prayer, not rote prayer, changes lives. And it does so, not because of anything we do and not because of a system or a method, but because it has everything to do with the importance the Lord has in our life. Do we really want to know Him to the point that we want to hear?

One early morning years ago, as I sat on the corner of my couch with my Bible opened and my prayer journal in my lap, I was faced with my unbelief. My mentor had confronted me in love. She asked me why I hadn't trusted in the Lord and why I hadn't looked to Him to meet my needs. I thought for a moment. Was I putting my trust in God and God alone? Did I look to Him for all of my needs? Was He truly my Lord? Was I listening to Him? No. There had been little desire to truly listen and obey. Why? I didn't really want to hear what He had to say. When I would pray I didn't want to listen too closely because I might hear something I did NOT want to hear. Knowingly and unknowingly I had shut the Lord out. I had pushed Him away. The result? Loneliness. Stark loneliness. I couldn't hear Him really at all. If we don't listen to Him in everything, we are not likely to hear Him in anything.

Think for a moment and ask yourself, "Am I listening to Him? Is He truly my Lord? Who is my all in all? Where am I putting my trust?" Do not be afraid. Answer honestly. You may think that I am talking to non-believers. Although we Christians already have Christ and are united with Him intimately, we need to learn to live out that relationship with Him. We want to know and walk in the joy of a true relationship. Lay yourself before Him, fix your eyes upon Him, and pour out your heart to Him. Draw near to God. Listen to His voice. Listen to Him and His will for you. And experience the sweet friendship and the sweet communion of oneness with Him. He will be who He already is—your best friend, your very best friend, your covenant Lord, your God, your all in all, and you will want to bring every request before Him. There will be nothing that you won't share with Him. There will be nothing that you won't ask Him first. Because He is your God and you are His beloved.

Interacting with God and His Word

Let's practice and think through the aspects of prayer we learned about today. Again, feel free to write your thoughts or answers to any questions in this section in a prayer journal or in the space provided at the end of the chapter.

ADORATION

Psalm 66:1-4

1   Shout for joy to God, all the earth;
2   sing the glory of his name;
        give to him glorious praise!
3   Say to God, "How awesome are your deeds!
        So great is your power that your enemies come cringing
        to you.
4   All the earth worships you
        and sings praises to you;
        they sing praises to your name."   *Selah*

Ask yourself, "Lord, do I praise you and worship you throughout my day? What are my thoughts and attitudes really like? How does my focus affect what I do and say?"

CONFESSION

Psalm 38:1-3

1   O LORD, rebuke me not in your anger,
        nor discipline me in your wrath!
2   For your arrows have sunk into me,
        and your hand has come down on me.
3   There is no soundness in my flesh
        because of your indignation;
    there is no health in my bones
        because of my sin.

Read the following questions and answer them as specifically and honestly as you can.

- Are you consumed by what others think of you?
- Are you concerned that you aren't measuring up?
- Do you feel the need to be perfect?
- Are you distracted by television, the internet, shopping?
- Are you feeling sorry for yourself?
- Are you frightened? Afraid? Worried?
- Are you able to identify the root of your sinful actions, words, or thoughts? Have you been able to see the things that trigger your ungodly thinking or behavior? (For additional help, refer to the "Ask Yourself" pages in the Appendix.) Maybe you are just beginning to see the anxiousness you feel, the worries that plague you, or the fear you live with as sin.

Make note of your observations in your prayer journal or in the space at the end of the chapter.

THANKSGIVING

Psalm 107:1-3

1   Oh give thanks to the LORD, for he is good,
        for his steadfast love endures forever!
2   Let the redeemed of the LORD say so,
        whom he has redeemed from trouble
3   and gathered in from the lands,
        from the east and from the west,
        from the north and from the south.

Thank God for all He has given to you in Christ. Thank Him for all He has done to provide for you. Thank Him for how you have seen Him show His love and kindness to you and to those in your life. Thank Him now for all He has done, is doing, and is going to do. Write your list of thanks in your prayer journal or in the space at the end of the chapter.

Search My Heart, O God

Prayerfully read all of Psalm 139 today. Write your thoughts or answers to any questions in this section in a prayer journal or in the space provided at the end of the chapter.

Psalm 139

1 O Lord, you have searched me and known me!
2 You know when I sit down and when I rise up;
     you discern my thoughts from afar.
3 You search out my path and my lying down
     and are acquainted with all my ways.
4 Even before a word is on my tongue,
     behold, O Lord, you know it altogether.
5 You hem me in, behind and before,
     and lay your hand upon me.
6 Such knowledge is too wonderful for me;
     it is high; I cannot attain it.

7 Where shall I go from your Spirit?
     Or where shall I flee from your presence?
8 If I ascend to heaven, you are there!
     If I make my bed in Sheol, you are there!
9 If I take the wings of the morning
     and dwell in the uttermost parts of the sea,
10 even there your hand shall lead me,
     and your right hand shall hold me.
11 If I say, "Surely the darkness shall cover me,
     and the light about me be night,"
12 even the darkness is not dark to you;
     the night is bright as the day,
     for darkness is as light with you.

13 For you formed my inward parts;
     you knitted me together in my mother's womb.

14 I praise you, for I am fearfully and wonderfully made.
    Wonderful are your works;
    my soul knows it very well.

15 My frame was not hidden from you,
    when I was being made in secret,
    intricately woven in the depths of the earth.

16 Your eyes saw my unformed substance;
    in your book were written, every one of them,
      the days that were formed for me,
      when as yet there was none of them.

17 How precious to me are your thoughts, O God!
    How vast is the sum of them!

18 If I would count them, they are more than the sand.
    I awake, and I am still with you.

19 Oh that you would slay the wicked, O God!
    O men of blood, depart from me!

20 They speak against you with malicious intent;
    your enemies take your name in vain.

21 Do I not hate those who hate you, O LORD?
    And do I not loathe those who rise up against you?

22 I hate them with complete hatred;
    I count them my enemies.

23 Search me, O God, and know my heart!
    Try me and know my thoughts!

24 And see if there be any grievous way in me,
    and lead me in the way everlasting!

Ask the Lord to help you observe your actions and your words this week. What would someone see of your heart? As you do this, remember Jesus' words from Matthew 11:28-30, calling you to come to Him: "Come to me, all who labor and are heavy laden, and I will give you rest. Take my yoke upon you, and learn from me, for I am gentle and lowly in heart, and you will find rest for your souls. For my yoke is easy, and my burden is light."

Laurie Aker

Close in ACTS Prayer

Adoration - Praise God for Who He Is

Confession - Admit Your Sins with a Repentant Heart

Thanksgiving - Thank God for All He Has Done, Is Doing, and Is Going to Do

Supplication - Make Your Requests to God for Yourself and On Behalf of Others.

Notes

Notes

CHAPTER 4

Ask the Father in My Name

After some time of asking God Most High, the creator of the universe, to search your innermost being, it may be appropriate to ask how you are doing. I am concerned about you. What has it been like to have Him probe into the darkness of your heart and soul with His eternal light? Are you feeling very vulnerable and wondering now, "What am I to do?" I imagine He has begun to reveal some of your wrong thinking, bad attitudes, and ungodly behaviors. As mentioned a couple weeks ago, you may be feeling discouraged, overwhelmed, or even in despair. If you are experiencing some of these feelings, please be encouraged. Listen again to Jesus' words: "Come to me, all who labor and are heavy laden, and I will give you rest. Take my yoke upon you, and learn from me, for I am gentle and lowly in heart, and you will find rest for your souls. For my yoke is easy, and my burden is light" (Matthew 11:28-30). And listen also to the apostle Paul, who stood by and watched Stephen be stoned to death: "There is therefore now no condemnation for those who are in Christ Jesus" (Romans 8:1).

This is a perfect time to again turn our focus to prayer and bring our heavy burdens before the Lord. Prayer is one of the greatest gifts the Lord has given to us. It is absolutely essential, and the Lord requires it of us. It is our part of the sanctification process. Jesus tells us that whatever we ask in His name He will do it. But even with this promise and even knowing that He desires us to come to Him, we too often don't believe and don't come. We try to handle things on our own. James admonishes us in his epistle: "You desire and do not have, so you murder. You covet and cannot obtain, so you fight and quarrel. You do not have, because you do not ask" (James 4:2). Prayer plus faith is our very conduit to the grace and power and mercy of God.

Last week we focused on many aspects of prayer and learned how to approach God in a godly context and how to establish an intimate relationship with Him through praise, confession, thanksgiving, and listening. This week we will add *supplication* as we continue to look at developing our relationship with Him through prayer. Supplication is the process of making a humble and earnest plea before God on our own behalf and on behalf of others. Due to the nature of this particular study, we will be focusing on the development of entreating the Lord on our own behalf. Charles Spurgeon said:

> Our responsibility is to go after the help that is provided for us: We must not sit still in despondency, but stir ourselves. Prayer will bring us quickly into the presence of our royal brother. Once before His throne we have only to ask and receive. His stores are not exhausted; there is still grain: His heart is not hard; He will give the grain to us. Lord, forgive our unbelief, and this evening constrain us to draw largely from Your fullness and receive grace for grace.[3]

What you learn to do well for yourself in prayer will significantly improve your compassion and understanding when you seek the Lord on behalf of your family and others. So before we go further with supplication, we want to first understand what we have been given so that we can make the most of this extravagant gift. We want to develop an effective and efficient prayer life by establishing a framework of faith in our mind and heart to build upon. How we view prayer and its effectiveness radically impacts our prayer life and our ability to go to God on our own behalf. This is extremely important. Let me put it another way: what we think and what we believe radically impacts what we do. So, if we don't believe prayer is the lifeline in our relationship with the Lord or if we don't believe prayer really impacts anything (or at least not in a personal way), then we won't be inclined to do it or to do it sincerely and with anticipation. Prayer is vitally important; it is a pivotal ingredient in our journey of moving our hearts from sinful to Spirit-filled. Make no mistake: God is the one who is in control and the one who does the work, but He has entrusted us with the "work" of prayer by faith.

There are three key pillars to all prayer. First, we must place our trust in the name and person of Jesus Christ. His name represents His character and who He is. Second, prayer must be built upon the truth of God's Word and obedience to that Word. Third, we must have an unwavering belief in the power of the one we pray to and His blessing of our prayers. These three pillars must be anchored in the foundation of a humble and contrite heart that understands there is nothing we can do apart from God, that He and He alone is the one who accomplishes all things by His power. He is the true sovereign God who reigns. It is He that is able to do all things, and with Him nothing is impossible. We will be transformed.

Pillar One: Trust in the name and person of Jesus. It is through Christ and Christ alone that we are able to approach God Most High. In Him, we have complete and unlimited access to the throne of God. When we confess our sinfulness, surrender our sin-filled life to Christ, and receive Christ's sinless life, we are given a whole new position. We are now in Christ, one with Him, and in His name we are able to go boldly into the Holy of Holies before God. But it's even more than that. Jesus becomes our covenant Lord, our tender shepherd, and our devoted advocate. He is for us and not against us. As our covenant Lord, He is our king who subdues our sin, protects us, and brings us to share in His inheritance, identity, and His position at the right hand of God. As a tender, loving shepherd He leads us with perfect love, knowledge, wisdom, and understanding: "The LORD is my shepherd; I shall not want. He makes me lie down in green pastures. He leads me beside still waters. He restores my soul. He leads me in paths of righteousness for his name's sake" (Psalm 23:1-3). As a devoted advocate He forever intercedes before the throne of God on our behalf. He not only knows what is best for us, but He has the power to bring it to pass.

Pillar Two: Trust in and obedience to the truth of God's Word. We are products of our culture and our environment, whether we want to be or not. And without even being aware of it, we have developed preconceived ideas about many things. There is every manner of unbelief and human thinking embedded in our hearts. However, as we immerse ourselves in God's Word and align our thinking and approach to prayer according to the truth of His Word, we will instead develop a godly, holy perspective and an extremely powerful and effective prayer life.

As hard as it may be, we need to trust God and His Word and believe to our very core that it is truth, the one and only truth. As we ask Him to search our hearts, we need to *listen* for the answer. And when he reveals any darkness, we can ask Him to help us really see what He shows us. It isn't easy to see our sin as God sees our sin. But we need to put our fears and our resistance aside, trust Him, and walk in obedience to His Word. We need to die to ourselves and become completely His. When we stand before Him one day, we want to offer to Him a pleasing sacrifice— ourselves! We are to do this even now (Romans 1-12). Listen to Paul's plea in Romans 12:1-2: I appeal to you therefore, brothers, by the mercies of God, to present your bodies as a living sacrifice, holy and acceptable to God, which is your spiritual worship. Do not be conformed to this world, but be transformed by the renewal of your mind, that by testing you may discern what is the will of God, what is good and acceptable and perfect." We need to remember and trust in the truths from God's Word: "Perfect love casts out all fear" (1 John 4:18); "There is therefore now no condemnation for those who are in Christ Jesus," (Romans 8:1); and "If we confess our sins, he is faithful and just to forgive us our sins and to cleanse us from all unrighteousness" (1 John 1:9).

Pillar Three: Faith in the power of Him who hears our prayers. We are unable to offer ourselves as a living sacrifice in our own strength. We need God's help. He will do it if only we will ask. Ask Him anything in His name and He will do it! When we ask according to His Word and when we are in Christ, we can be confident that He will answer our prayer. It may not happen as we expect, it may not be when we expect, and it may not be what we want, but He will do it.

The more we trust Him and follow Him in absolute obedience, the more beautiful and glorifying the outcome. Faith, trust, and obedience are essential components to bring about transformation. They are key ingredients in our pursuit of holiness and in our sanctification. Nothing is more pleasing to God than when we follow Him fully, by faith, trusting Him and obeying Him as we go. It is the sweetest fragrance to Him, and He wants to bless us for it. Jesus told the crowd in the Sermon on the Mount, "Blessed are the pure in heart, for they shall see God" (Matthew 5:8). We won't see God face to face until we are in heaven, but when we follow Him by faith, trusting in Him, we see His hand at work! I have grown to cherish prayer more and more because the Lord pulls back the veil and lets us see more of Him when we pray. Other than pleasing my Lord and Savior, seeing Him more clearly is one of the greatest, if not the greatest, treasures this side of heaven. I also believe when we hear God's voice and see the results of our time alone with Him, we can serve as better witnesses to the world around us. There is something different about those who really walk with Jesus and spend time in His presence. They are bolder, more confident, and more able to keep their eyes fixed upon Him and not on the things of this world: "Now when they saw the boldness of Peter and John, and perceived that they were uneducated, common men, they were astonished. And they recognized that they had been with Jesus" (Acts 4:13).

In Psalm 37 David instructs us to not fret or be afraid but to delight ourselves in the Lord, to trust in Him and witness His response as our Lord, shepherd, and advocate.

Interacting with God and His Word

Read Psalm 86. Write your thoughts or answers to any questions in this section in a prayer journal or in the space provided at the end of the chapter.

Psalm 86

1   Incline your ear, O Lord, and answer me,
        for I am poor and needy.
2   Preserve my life, for I am godly;
        save your servant, who trusts in you—you are my God.

3   Be gracious to me, O Lord,
        for to you do I cry all the day.
4   Gladden the soul of your servant,
        for to you, O Lord, do I lift up my soul.
5   For you, O Lord, are good and forgiving,
        abounding in steadfast love to all who call upon you.
6   Give ear, O Lord, to my prayer;
        listen to my plea for grace.
7   In the day of my trouble I call upon you,
        for you answer me.

8   There is none like you among the gods, O Lord,
        nor are there any works like yours.
9   All the nations you have made shall come
        and worship before you, O Lord,
        and shall glorify your name.
10 For you are great and do wondrous things;
        you alone are God.
11 Teach me your way, O Lord,
        that I may walk in your truth;
        unite my heart to fear your name.
12 I give thanks to you, O Lord my God, with my whole heart,
        and I will glorify your name forever.
13 For great is your steadfast love toward me;
        you have delivered my soul from the depths of Sheol.

14 O God, insolent men have risen up against me;
        a band of ruthless men seeks my life,
        and they do not set you before them.
15 But you, O Lord, are a God merciful and gracious,
        slow to anger and abounding in steadfast love and faithfulness.
16 Turn to me and be gracious to me;
        give your strength to your servant,
        and save the son of your maidservant.
17 Show me a sign of your favor,
        that those who hate me may see and be put to shame
        because you, Lord, have helped me and comforted me.

How does David approach God? What does he do with his burdens, his heartaches, and his concerns? What does he ask God?

Daniel was a man who trusted in God, whose prayers were built upon the truth of God's Word and faith in the power and privilege of prayer. From them we will learn about the privilege of supplication: how to bring our requests before the Lord and from what posture we should bring them. Read Daniel 6:6-28.

Daniel 6:6-28

Then these high officials and satraps came by agreement to the king and said to him, "O King Darius, live forever! 7 All the high officials of the kingdom, the prefects and the satraps, the counselors and the governors are agreed that the king should establish an ordinance and enforce an injunction, that whoever makes petition to any god or man for thirty days, except to you, O king, shall be cast into the den of lions. 8 Now, O king, establish the injunction and sign the document, so that it cannot be changed, according to the law of the Medes and the Persians, which cannot be revoked." 9 Therefore King Darius signed the document and injunction.

10 When Daniel knew that the document had been signed, he went to his house where he had windows in his upper chamber open toward Jerusalem. He got down on his knees three times a day and prayed and gave thanks before his God, as he had done previously. 11 Then these men came by agreement and found Daniel making petition and plea before his God. 12 Then they came near and said before the king, concerning the injunction, "O king! Did you not sign an injunction, that anyone who makes petition to any god or man within thirty days except to you, O king, shall be cast into the den of lions?" The king answered and said, "The thing stands fast, according to the law of the Medes and Persians, which cannot be revoked." 13 Then they answered and

said before the king, "Daniel, who is one of the exiles from Judah, pays no attention to you, O king, or the injunction you have signed, but makes his petition three times a day."

14 Then the king, when he heard these words, was much distressed and set his mind to deliver Daniel. And he labored till the sun went down to rescue him.15 Then these men came by agreement to the king and said to the king, "Know, O king, that it is a law of the Medes and Persians that no injunction or ordinance that the king establishes can be changed."

16 Then the king commanded, and Daniel was brought and cast into the den of lions. The king declared to Daniel, "May your God, whom you serve continually, deliver you!" 17 And a stone was brought and laid on the mouth of the den, and the king sealed it with his own signet and with the signet of his lords, that nothing might be changed concerning Daniel. 18 Then the king went to his palace and spent the night fasting; no diversions were brought to him, and sleep fled from him.

19 Then, at break of day, the king arose and went in haste to the den of lions. 20 As he came near to the den where Daniel was, he cried out in a tone of anguish. The king declared to Daniel, "O Daniel, servant of the living God, has your God, whom you serve continually, been able to deliver you from the lions?" 21 Then Daniel said to the king, "O king, live forever! 22 My God sent his angel and shut the lions' mouths, and they have not harmed me, because I was found blameless before him; and also before you, O king, I have done no harm." 23 Then the king was exceedingly glad, and commanded that Daniel be taken up out of the den. So Daniel was taken up out of the den, and no kind of harm was found on him, because he had trusted in his God. 24 And the king commanded, and those men who had maliciously accused Daniel were brought and cast into the den of lions—they,

their children, and their wives. And before they reached the bottom of the den, the lions overpowered them and broke all their bones in pieces.

25 Then King Darius wrote to all the peoples, nations, and languages that dwell in all the earth: "Peace be multiplied to you. 26 I make a decree, that in all my royal dominion people are to tremble and fear before the God of Daniel,

for he is the living God,
enduring forever;
his kingdom shall never be destroyed,
and his dominion shall be to the end.
27 He delivers and rescues;
he works signs and wonders
in heaven and on earth,
he who has saved Daniel
from the power of the lions."

28 So this Daniel prospered during the reign of Darius and the reign of Cyrus the Persian.

What does this passage say about Daniel and his prayer life? Think about his commitment to prayer. Daniel's trial is different than the trials you may face during the day. Your challenge may be sleeplessness, your to-do list that "must" get done, or the constant demands of little ones. Would you take a moment to ask the Lord to help you, by His grace, in His power, to be fully committed and consistent in prayer, no matter what trials or obstacles you face each day?

As you reflect on how Daniel responded, what are you doing now that reflects your hope and trust in God? What needs to change in your thinking about prayer and about your daily schedule in order that your heart would be aligned to God's Word?

Search My Heart, O God

Prayerfully read the following excerpts from Psalm 139. As you pray, ask the Lord to help you again "see" what you are thinking—the thought processes and feelings behind your actions. (Again, refer to the "Ask Yourself" pages in the Appendix for additional help.) Ask the Lord to give you wisdom. As you boldly continue to ask God to search your heart and as He continues to reveal those deep and hidden things to you, choose to bring them before the throne. Jot down any thoughts from this section in a prayer journal or in the space provided at the end of the chapter.

Psalm 139

1 O LORD, you have searched me and known me!
2 You know when I sit down and when I rise up;
      you discern my thoughts from afar.
3 You search out my path and my lying down
      and are acquainted with all my ways.
4 Even before a word is on my tongue,
      behold, O LORD, you know it altogether.
5 You hem me in, behind and before,
      and lay your hand upon me.
6 Such knowledge is too wonderful for me;
      it is high; I cannot attain it.

13 For you formed my inward parts;
      you knitted me together in my mother's womb.
14 I praise you, for I am fearfully and wonderfully made.
   Wonderful are your works;
      my soul knows it very well.
15 My frame was not hidden from you,
      when I was being made in secret,
         intricately woven in the depths of the earth.
16 Your eyes saw my unformed substance;
    in your book were written, every one of them,
      the days that were formed for me,
      when as yet there was none of them.

23 Search me, O God, and know my heart!
      Try me and know my thoughts!
24 And see if there be any grievous way in me,
      and lead me in the way everlasting!

Close in ACTS Prayer

Adoration - Praise God for Who He Is

Confession - Admit Your Sins with a Repentant Heart

Thanksgiving - Thank God for All He Has Done, Is Doing, and Is Going to Do

Supplication - Make Your Requests to God for Yourself and On Behalf of Others.

Notes

CHAPTER 5

A Holy Fast: Fasting to Feast

Fasting is not really in fashion in the Christian realm today. Denying self, picking up one's cross, waiting, doing without—none of these things are particularly "en vogue." Many people might fast or diet to lose weight, to look better, or to be healthier and some might exercise to have the *right* body, but it is rather rare to hear of someone fasting and even more rare to hear that someone fasts as a part of his or her regular Christian discipline. Subconsciously, people can resist the idea of having a structured and disciplined regimen of prayer, fasting, and Bible study in their lives, calling it legalistic. Yet at the same time they can be caught up in measuring their holiness or the holiness of others depending upon what kind of music they listen to, which school their children attend, what clothes they wear, or how much they volunteer. We want to be so careful and prayerful as we hunger after the holiness of God to remain in a posture of humility, keeping our eyes fixed upon Him. He alone is God, and it is His mercy and grace that imparts righteousness to us. We can do nothing to earn it, buy it, or bribe Him for it, or it wouldn't be grace. Grace is God's unmerited favor, poured out upon us by His hand, and His hand alone.

"Truly, truly, I say to you, unless you eat the flesh of the Son of Man and drink his blood, you have no life in you" (John 6:53). Jesus calls us to come to Him by faith, die to our sinful selves, and receive His righteous life. Once we have made that great exchange, how do we continue in pursuit of holiness? How do we seek to be filled with Him and be emptied of self? We must continue to feast upon Him, to eat of the flesh of the Son of God and drink His blood through humble, faith-filled, and diligent study of the Bible, prayer, and fasting. This is what God desires of us. What other way could it possibly be done?

We want to focus on fasting—what it means and how to put it into practice—for the purpose of discovering what lies within our hearts and rooting out those things that are not of God. Andrew Murray identifies the purpose of fasting clearly and concisely: "Fasting helps to express, to deepen, and to confirm the resolution that we are ready to sacrifice anything, even ourselves, to attain the kingdom."[4] Richard Foster declares, " … more than any other discipline, fasting reveals the things that control us."[5] Fasting from food or any cherished thing is intentionally pushing ourselves away from our full plates of self and setting our hearts at the banquet table of the Lord, seeking to feast upon Him and only Him. Paul proclaims, "Indeed, I count everything as loss because of the surpassing worth of knowing Christ Jesus my Lord. For his sake I have suffered the loss of all things and count them as rubbish, in order that I may gain Christ" (Philippians 3:8).

When we fast and when we make it a point to fast regularly, we are communicating with our souls and with our bodies that we truly desire to see a work of God. We are laying ourselves prostrate before His throne, crying out to Him for His mercy to do a work in us that only He can do. We are demonstrating in word and deed that we know we can do nothing apart from God. We are acknowledging that all good things come from His hand, even our ability to fast. We are appealing to Him to gently reveal to us whom or what we truly treasure.

How much do you desire God? How much do you desire to see a work of God in your heart? How much do you believe that He is the only thing that truly satisfies? How much do you believe that only He can accomplish anything of eternal value?

I am going to ask you to fast, but not until the next chapter. For now, focus on allowing the Lord to prepare the soil of your heart to fast. So, as you prepare to begin fasting, know that you are practicing a very important discipline, one that is humble and glorifying to God. Disciplines like this are what the Lord has given to us to do. By faith, we are to "work out [our] own salvation with fear and trembling" (Philippians 2:12). We are doing what only we can do as we ask God to do what only He can do. "Was not Abraham our father justified by works when he offered up his son Isaac on the altar? You see that faith was active along with his works, and faith was completed by his works; and the Scripture was fulfilled that says, 'Abraham believed God, and it was counted to him as righteousness—and he was called a friend of God'" (James 2:21-23).

As you fast, you are appealing to God to do what you know only He can do. You are proclaiming He is God and you are not and imploring Him to render your heart pliable and moldable. You are bowing before Him in your wretchedness and asking Him to open your ears to hear Him and your eyes to see your sin as He sees your sin. We need our loving gardener to plow and till our souls. As the clay lies beholden to the potter, we lie awaiting the move of our beloved Lord.

Although fasting is work, it is sacrifice and it is self-abasement and self-denial. We are saying we are nothing apart from Christ. We are saying we need Him and that He is life. Man does not live by bread alone but by every word that proceeds from the mouth of God (Deuteronomy 8:3). Ultimately, fasting is truly feasting. Jesus is our true food. We must remember this or we will lose the focus of the fast. Feast fully upon Him and rejoice!

Take time today to make a list of the temporal things that are enjoyable to you, things like food, drink, sleep, sex, television, or reading. Before anything, spend time in prayer. Write your prayer as you seek the Lord, asking Him what would be the appropriate fast for you at this time, how much, and for how long. You may feel led to give up lunch each day and spend that time with the Lord in His Word. You may feel led to sleep one half hour less in the morning because you love those last moments of sleep. God may be leading you to go without food for a 24-hour period once a week. He may lead you to go without your favorite coffee or soda for a month. Seek the Lord. Seek His face and His perfect will. We all are wired differently, and at different times in our lives different things are important or appropriate. The late Martyn Lloyd-Jones said:

> Fasting, if we conceive of it truly, must not ... be confined to the question of food and drink; fasting should really be made to include abstinence from anything which is legitimate in and of itself for the sake of some special spiritual purpose. There are many bodily functions which are right and normal and perfectly legitimate, but which for special peculiar reasons in certain circumstances should be controlled. That is fasting.[6]

In Matthew 6:16-18 Jesus said:

> And when you fast, do not look gloomy like the hypocrites, for they disfigure their faces that their fasting may be seen by others. Truly, I say to you, they have received their reward. But when you fast, anoint your head and wash your face, that your fasting may not be seen by others but by your Father who is in secret. And your Father who sees in secret will reward you.

For more examples of fasting in the Bible, please see Exodus 34:28; Leviticus 16:29, 23:32; Deuteronomy 9:9-18; 2 Samuel 12:15-20; Esther 4:12-17; Daniel 1, 10:2; Matthew 4:1-11.

Interacting with God and His Word

Read the following excerpts from Psalm 40 and Psalm 63. Write your thoughts or answers to any questions in this section in a prayer journal or in the space provided at the end of the chapter.

Psalm 40:1-5

1   I waited patiently for the Lord;
         he inclined to me and heard my cry.
2   He drew me up from the pit of destruction,
         out of the miry bog,
         and set my feet upon a rock,
         making my steps secure.

3 He put a new song in my mouth,
      a song of praise to our God.
   Many will see and fear,
      and put their trust in the Lord.
4 Blessed is the man who makes
      the Lord his trust,
   who does not turn to the proud,
      to those who go astray after a lie!
5 You have multiplied, O Lord my God,
      your wondrous deeds and your thoughts toward us;
      none can compare with you!
   I will proclaim and tell of them,
      yet they are more than can be told.

Psalm 63:1-8

1 O God, you are my God; earnestly I seek you;
      my soul thirsts for you;
   my flesh faints for you,
      as in a dry and weary land where there is no water.
2 So I have looked upon you in the sanctuary,
      beholding your power and glory.
3 Because your steadfast love is better than life,
      my lips will praise you.
4 So I will bless you as long as I live;
      in your name I will lift up my hands.

5 My soul will be satisfied as with fat and rich food,
      and my mouth will praise you with joyful lips,
6 when I remember you upon my bed,
      and meditate on you in the watches of the night;
7 for you have been my help,
      and in the shadow of your wings I will sing for joy.
8 My soul clings to you;
      your right hand upholds me.

Just like Daniel, turn to the Lord with all your heart: "Then I turned my face to the Lord God, seeking him by prayer and pleas for mercy with fasting and sackcloth and ashes" (Daniel 9:3). Ask the Lord to help you seek after Him with all of your heart just as David asked in Psalm 63:1.

Search My Heart, O God

Prayerfully read the following excerpts from Psalm 139.

Psalm 139

7   Where shall I go from your Spirit?
        Or where shall I flee from your presence?
8   If I ascend to heaven, you are there!
        If I make my bed in Sheol, you are there!
9   If I take the wings of the morning
        and dwell in the uttermost parts of the sea,
10 even there your hand shall lead me,
        and your right hand shall hold me.
11 If I say, "Surely the darkness shall cover me,
        and the light about me be night,"
12 even the darkness is not dark to you;
        the night is bright as the day,
        for darkness is as light with you.

17 How precious to me are your thoughts, O God!
        How vast is the sum of them!
18 If I would count them, they are more than the sand.
        I awake, and I am still with you.

23 Search me, O God, and know my heart!
        Try me and know my thoughts!
24 And see if there be any grievous way in me,
        and lead me in the way everlasting!

As you boldly ask God to search your heart and as He continues to reveal those deep and hidden things to you, choose to bring them before the throne. Ask Him to help you observe your actions, your words, your thoughts, and your attitude. As you pay attention to the things that continue to "pop" into your head, jot them down. Is there fear? Is there worry? Is there concern for what others might think? Is there difficulty understanding God's ways and trusting Him? Be honest. Be real. Don't hold back and don't try to carry these thoughts on your own. Ask God to give you His truth to replace your wrong thinking. He will!

You might want to consider finding two or three Scriptures that specifically target the sin you are observing. For instance, if you continue to observe "worry," look up *worry* in a concordance or online Bible (like BibleGateway.com) and choose verses that best describe your wrong thinking. Try writing these verses in your prayer journal, typing them in the notes on your smartphone, and/or writing them on a 3x5 card to meditate on or memorize and to be able to recall in moments of worry.

Close in ACTS Prayer

Adoration - Praise God for Who He Is

Confession - Admit Your Sins with a Repentant Heart

Thanksgiving - Thank God for All He Has Done, Is Doing, and Is Going to Do

Supplication - Make Your Requests to God for Yourself and On Behalf of Others.

Notes

CHAPTER 6

Repentance: A Posture of Humility

Not unlike the old adage, one rotten apple destroys the whole bunch, sin left unattended in our hearts will slowly corrupt the entire heart and then compromise the whole body. The Bible puts it this way, "Either make the tree good, and its fruit good; or make the tree bad, and its fruit bad; for the tree is known by its fruit. You brood of vipers, how can you, being evil, speak what is good? For the mouth speaks out of that which fills the heart. The good man out of his good treasure brings forth what is good; and the evil man out of his evil treasure brings forth what is evil," (Matthew 12:33-35). You cannot draw fresh water from a contaminated well; you cannot harvest righteousness from unrighteousness.

We must carefully tend our hearts. When we have been given the awesome, magnificent, and merciful gift of eternal life, and our hearts are transferred from the kingdom of darkness to the kingdom of life, we must care for our hearts with deep gratitude and devotion. I was reminded of the importance of caring for our hearts in a very visual way several years ago. An old man had passed away, and I was asked to accompany a relative as they sorted through their uncle's belongings at his estate. The home had been built in a very affluent neighborhood of Chicago by the grandfather of the person I was accompanying. As we drove up and parked in the driveway, I was shocked. It hadn't been cared for in years. As we entered the once beautiful house, I was horrified. I had never seen anything like it. There were hundreds and hundreds of cobwebs hanging from the ceilings that clung to my shoulders and face as we walked through the house. I tried to brush them out of the way, but they would then tangle themselves around my arms. A maze of boxes overwhelmed the entire house, resulting in only a narrow passageway in each room through which to walk. There were papers, dishes, boxes and magazines everywhere. It was clear these things had been there no less than ten or fifteen years. We had to squeeze our way through the darkness because all of the lights were burnt out. With each step my stomach turned as the flashlight illuminated the carpet below crawling with insects. The bedroom where the old man had slept and the bathroom he had used were indescribable. The rest of the upstairs was so filled with boxes we couldn't even get in. The old man who lived in the house had lost his mother many years earlier and had lived alone since then. His parents had left the home to him in their will. It was clear he had done no housekeeping or maintenance. This home, carefully designed and well appointed with fine paneling, carpets and cabinetry, had been carelessly treated and left to ruin.

Walking through this home I felt as though I was being dragged through every nook and cranny of a sin-infested heart, a heart that had been left unchecked for the course of a lifetime. Sadly, I, too, knew this man. He was my uncle as well. I remembered the conversations my father had with him over the years, encouraging him to take care of the home that their dad built. He often offered to come and help my uncle, because my dad had been a carpenter in his youth. Yet, my uncle refused. He was set in his ways and wouldn't change. He spent his time and his money on frivolous things, eating out, and visiting museums. His sin was so clearly manifested in what little was left of his home, a home now in ruins and filled with filth. I stared in motionless nausea at the rooms ravaged by neglect, a picture of self-centered and myopic living. Shortly thereafter, the home had to be leveled to the ground; the treasured memory of my grandfather gone forever.

My uncle had been given a wonderful gift, but he never took care of it. In Christ we have been given a marvelous, priceless gift. We have been given new hearts (Ezekiel 36:25-27), and we need to tend them with great care. I am certain that most of you, if not all of you, take good care of your homes, but what if someone were to knock on the front door of your heart and you had to let them in for a walk-through this afternoon? What would they find in the nooks and crannies? What has been shut up in your heart, presumably hidden where no one can see? Or can they? Can the Lord?

The wellspring of life flows from our hearts (Proverbs 4:23). What we allow to harbor there affects our entire being. Our lifeblood flows through that heart. If it is infested, our whole system is infested. What about your heart? What lies beneath the surface? What hides behind the curtain? In the drawer? Under the bed? In the grout?

The more I understand the far-reaching effects of sin, the more I want to be willing to do whatever is necessary to get at the root. Repentance is one of the tools the Lord has given to us to help us root out the sin. We want to live in a posture of repentance. Once we have seen our sinfulness and our wretchedness and seen His mercy, and once we have laid down every part of our sinful lives at His feet and received His perfect righteousness in return, we must continue walking forward in that posture of humility.

Repentance means we must stop—stop doing what we are doing and turn from our sinful ways to His righteous ways. By God's grace, through the power of the Holy Spirit, we must confess our sin and turn from it. We must stop doing what we normally do; we must get at the sin and remove the root. Then we must replace the root of unrighteousness with the root of righteousness, the seed of righteousness. This week we will look at repentance and practice it. The gardener first must remove the weeds in the soil before he can plant the seed he desires to harvest!

Interacting with God and His Word

When we confess our sin, God forgives our sin. We can go forward and He will instruct us in the way of repentance. Let's read Psalm 32. As you complete this section, remember to write your thoughts or answers to any questions in this section in a prayer journal or in the space provided at the end of the chapter.

Psalm 32

1   Blessed is the one whose transgression is forgiven,
     whose sin is covered.
2   Blessed is the man against whom the Lord counts no iniquity,
     and in whose spirit there is no deceit.

3   For when I kept silent, my bones wasted away
     through my groaning all day long.
4   For day and night your hand was heavy upon me;
     my strength was dried up as by the heat of summer. *Selah*

5   I acknowledged my sin to you,
     and I did not cover my iniquity;
    I said, "I will confess my transgressions to the Lord,"
     and you forgave the iniquity of my sin. *Selah*

6   Therefore let everyone who is godly
     offer prayer to you at a time when you may be found;
    surely in the rush of great waters,
     they shall not reach him.
7   You are a hiding place for me;
     you preserve me from trouble;
    you surround me with shouts of deliverance. *Selah*
8   I will instruct you and teach you in the way you should go;
     I will counsel you with my eye upon you.
9   Be not like a horse or a mule, without understanding,
     which must be curbed with bit and bridle,
    or it will not stay near you.

10 Many are the sorrows of the wicked,
     but steadfast love surrounds the one who trusts in the Lord.
11 Be glad in the Lord, and rejoice, O righteous,
     and shout for joy, all you upright in heart!

Jesus is not looking for people who appear good on the outside. He looks at the heart. He sees the heart and the deeds that come from it, and He is not deceived.

Matthew 12:33-35

Either make the tree good and its fruit good, or make the
tree bad and its fruit bad, for the tree is known by its fruit.
You brood of vipers! How can you speak good, when you
are evil? For out of the abundance of the heart the mouth
speaks. The good person out of his good treasure brings
forth good, and the evil person out of his evil treasure
brings forth evil.

Let us not be deceived; we will reap what we sow. Make it your priority
to call your sin what it is and turn from it. Don't be like the Pharisees who
knew all about how to look righteous, but on the inside were ravenous
wolves.

Revelation 2:5

Remember therefore from where you have fallen; repent,
and do the works you did at first. If not, I will come to
you and remove your lampstand from its place, unless
you repent.

Revelation 3:19

Those whom I love, I reprove and discipline; be zealous
therefore, and repent.

Ask yourself, "Do I have a repentant heart?" Take time to examine
your heart and continue to review the Scriptures you were instructed to
find in the last chapter—and seek others. We need to humble ourselves
before Him and repent of our pride. Instead of your normal prayer time
today, get up from where you are sitting right now and bow yourself before
Him, even prostrate yourself on the floor. Acknowledge to Him that He
knows what is best—that His timing and ways are perfect. Fall into His
will and His grace. We need to repent of our fear and our longing for
something other than His best and Him alone. Take time right now to lay
any doubts, insecurities, fears, and longings at His feet.

2 Corinthians 7:10-11

For godly grief produces a repentance that leads to salvation without regret, whereas worldly grief produces death. 11 For see what earnestness this godly grief has produced in you, but also what eagerness to clear yourselves, what indignation, what fear, what longing, what zeal, what punishment!

When you tell the Lord that you are sorry and ask Him to forgive you, is there change in your behavior? Do you stop doing what you were doing?

Search My Heart, O God

Prayerfully read the following excerpt from Psalm 139.

Psalm 139

13 For you formed my inward parts;
    you knitted me together in my mother's womb.
14 I praise you, for I am fearfully and wonderfully made.
    Wonderful are your works;
      my soul knows it very well.
15 My frame was not hidden from you,
    when I was being made in secret,
      intricately woven in the depths of the earth.
16 Your eyes saw my unformed substance;
    in your book were written, every one of them,
      the days that were formed for me,
      when as yet there was none of them.
17 How precious to me are your thoughts, O God!
    How vast is the sum of them!
18 If I would count them, they are more than the sand.
    I awake, and I am still with you.

23 Search me, O God, and know my heart!
    Try me and know my thoughts!

24 And see if there be any grievous way in me,
and lead me in the way everlasting!

Consider the ungodly actions, words, thoughts, or attitudes the Lord has revealed to you. Again, it might be helpful to gather two or three Scriptures that specifically target your root sin, such as worry, fear, or pride. You can look up verses in a concordance or online Bible (like BibleGateway.com) and choose a couple that best describe your wrong thinking. As you may have learned, it can be so helpful to write them in your prayer journal, in the notes on your smartphone, and/or on a 3x5 card to meditate on or memorize.

Now is also the time to initiate your fast, based on what you believe the Lord asked you to do as you prepared.

Close in ACTS Prayer

Adoration - Praise God for Who He Is

Confession - Admit Your Sins with a Repentant Heart

Thanksgiving - Thank God for All He Has Done, Is Doing, and Is Going to Do

Supplication - Make Your Requests to God for Yourself and On Behalf of Others.

Notes

CHAPTER 7

A Victory Garden: Planting Righteousness

Repentance means we must stop. Stop doing what we are doing and turn from our sinful ways to the Lord's righteous ways. But it also means we must go. We must go forward in the path of righteousness. Holy transformation doesn't mean that we just stop doing something; it means that we stop doing things our way, and instead, do them God's way. When we uproot the weeds, we need to be ready to plant something in their place. And we don't want to stop working until our garden is completely transformed and in full bloom! Then we will want to carefully tend it so that it will remain that way!

Envision with me for a moment a barren wasteland: crusty, dry, unforgiving, uninviting, uncomfortable, and hard, anything but nurturing and not conducive to any kind of growth. Now erase that image and replace it with another: a magnificent garden, one that seems to go on as far as the eye can see in every direction, full of color and rich greenery, winding paths, secluded benches, and rippling fountains. A full floral display is before you, and no matter which way you journey you are still in the midst of another world, saturated with color, fragrance, and beauty.

It's a place like no other. This is the image we want to reflect in our hearts. This full, lush garden will bloom within our hearts when we put off the old, repent from our sin, and allow the Holy Spirit to deeply till the soil within our hearts and plant the character and righteousness of Christ. As each area of our heart is rototilled, reclaimed, and replanted, our lives will pour forth the vibrant color, the sweet fragrance, and the everlasting beauty of Christ.

Don't be afraid to continue to look honestly at yourself, and don't be lazy with your sin. Be willing to ask help from your Lord, from a fellow sister in Christ, from your husband, or from a family member. Do whatever you can to identify the weeds so they can be uprooted and then replaced with the precious character of our Lord Jesus Christ.

So then, this week, be eager to plant a new crop. As you search the scriptures to find the righteous thinking to replace your ungodly thinking, be ready to share with your small group. Think of at least one friend that you can share with about the truth you desire to plant in place of the old lie that you have uprooted. Tell them what you are going to do and ask them to hold you accountable. Then be ready to watch the righteousness grow! Daily continue to tend to it and weed out any wrong thinking. Anticipate and look forward to the fruitful harvest, a great harvest of righteousness, for your Lord. Replanting our sin with a beautiful rose of righteousness is an incredible and extremely rewarding task. We are replacing the thorns of bitterness, selfishness, jealousy, or idolatry with the fragrant aroma and lovely blossoms of the Spirit: love, joy, peace, patience, kindness, goodness, faithfulness, gentleness, and self-control!

A wellspring. We speak more of who Christ is by who He is in us than anything we ever say or do. When you are filled with Him, He overflows out of you. He radiates from your smile, He shines forth from your eyes, His love emanates from your heart, and His care is demonstrated through your gentle touch and His comfort in your embrace. Our goal, our desire, and our vision should be to be a vessel that God uses to cause others to want to know Him more, to be brought to their knees in worship, to believe that He is the Christ, the Son of God, their Savior! In all that you do and in all that you are, may you tell them with and without words who He is! May they sense when they have been with you that not only have you been with Jesus, but that they feel they have been in His presence.

"But thanks be to God, who always leads us in triumph in Christ, and manifests through us the sweet aroma of the knowledge of Him in every place" (2 Cor. 2:14).

As our sinfulness is replaced by His righteousness, as our flesh is put to death and we are filled more and more with His Spirit, not only will we be blessed and be a blessing to others, we will be the sweet aroma of Christ, a garden of righteousness and holiness that may draw them closer to Christ himself. This is the gospel: "Not I, but Christ." But we live in a world that beats more to the drum of, "Not Christ, but me!" We say we are Christians and yet we serve self. If we want to have a true harvest of righteousness, we must labor for that harvest! Do not be deceived; an apple seed will only bring forth a harvest of apples. We will only reap what we sow! Let's sow unto righteousness and unto His glory! May we be a vision of His glory, a garden of victory over sin, a garden of righteousness!

Interacting with God and His Word

Psalm 139 ends with the plea, "Lead me in the way everlasting!" Listen to David praise God as his shepherd in Psalm 23.

Psalm 23

1   The Lord is my shepherd; I shall not want.
2   He makes me lie down in green pastures.
    He leads me beside still waters.
3   He restores my soul.
    He leads me in paths of righteousness
      for his name's sake.

4   Even though I walk through the valley of the shadow of death,
      I will fear no evil,
   for you are with me;
      your rod and your staff,
      they comfort me.
5   You prepare a table before me
      in the presence of my enemies;
   you anoint my head with oil;

> my cup overflows.
> 6 Surely goodness and mercy shall follow me
>> all the days of my life,
>>> and I shall dwell in the house of the Lord
>>>> forever.

Don't be afraid to ask Him to take you by the hand and show you how to respond rightly. We are sheep, and we need a shepherd continually to guide us and show us the way.

We walk in the law of the Lord by His Spirit. Read Psalm 119:1-6 and observe how we follow the Lord as our shepherd.

Psalm 119:1-6

> 1 Blessed are those whose way is blameless,
>> who walk in the law of the LORD!
> 2 Blessed are those who keep his testimonies,
>> who seek him with their whole heart,
> 3 who also do no wrong,
>> but walk in his ways!
> 4 You have commanded your precepts
>> to be kept diligently.
> 5 Oh that my ways may be steadfast
>> in keeping your statutes!
> 6 Then I shall not be put to shame,
>> having my eyes fixed on all your commandments.

We cannot make ourselves righteous by rule following; we are only righteous in Christ. However, when we confess and turn from our lukewarm ways and seek to faithfully obey the Lord in His Word—out of heartfelt gratitude for all He has done for us in Christ—we are doing what God asks us to do. He will do the rest, just as a seed planted in the garden. We can plant the seed and water it, but only God can make it grow (1 Corinthians 3:6-7).

Now read Psalm 119:7-32. When you come to a verse that is *not* true of you or your heart, confess that to the Lord right then and ask Him to forgive you and to replace your wrong attitude with His righteous attitude.

Ask yourself, "Are my eyes fixed on God's Word and His commandments? Are they always before me, a measurement for all I do?"

Psalm 119:7-32

7   I will praise you with an upright heart,
        when I learn your righteous rules.
8   I will keep your statutes;
        do not utterly forsake me!

9   How can a young man keep his way pure?
        By guarding it according to your word.
10 With my whole heart I seek you;
        let me not wander from your commandments!
11 I have stored up your word in my heart,
        that I might not sin against you.
12 Blessed are you, O LORD;
        teach me your statutes!
13 With my lips I declare
        all the rules of your mouth.
14 In the way of your testimonies I delight
        as much as in all riches.
15 I will meditate on your precepts
        and fix my eyes on your ways.
16 I will delight in your statutes;
        I will not forget your word.

17 Deal bountifully with your servant,
        that I may live and keep your word.
18 Open my eyes, that I may behold
        wondrous things out of your law.
19 I am a sojourner on the earth;
        hide not your commandments from me!
20 My soul is consumed with longing
        for your rules at all times.
21 You rebuke the insolent, accursed ones,
        who wander from your commandments.

22 Take away from me scorn and contempt,
  for I have kept your testimonies.
23 Even though princes sit plotting against me,
  your servant will meditate on your statutes.
24 Your testimonies are my delight;
  they are my counselors.

25 My soul clings to the dust;
  give me life according to your word!
26 When I told of my ways, you answered me;
  teach me your statutes!
27 Make me understand the way of your precepts,
  and I will meditate on your wondrous works.
28 My soul melts away for sorrow;
  strengthen me according to your word!
29 Put false ways far from me
  and graciously teach me your law!
30 I have chosen the way of faithfulness;
  I set your rules before me.
31 I cling to your testimonies, O LORD;
  let me not be put to shame!
32 I will run in the way of your commandments
  when you enlarge my heart!

Search My Heart, O God

Prayerfully read Psalm 139:17-18, 23-24 today.

Psalm 139

17 How precious to me are your thoughts, O God!
  How vast is the sum of them!
18 If I would count them, they are more than the sand.
  I awake, and I am still with you.

23 Search me, O God, and know my heart!
  Try me and know my thoughts!

24 And see if there be any grievous way in me,
 and lead me in the way everlasting!

Continue to allow the Lord to test you and try you and search every corner of your heart, remembering that He is good all the time and desires to make you like Jesus. As we desire to be led onto the path of righteousness, let's now find Scriptures that will help us replace our root of sin with a root of righteousness. Pray before you begin, asking God to show you the Scriptures you need to light your path and to address those things that need changing. For example, if you have found *pride* to be your stumbling block, you would replace it with *humility* and then look up Scriptures referring to humility, the humble, and humbling yourself before God Most High. If you are filled with *fear,* you would look up Scriptures about *faith* and replace your root of fear with the root of faith. As you work, by faith, to replace wrong thinking with biblical thinking, try to imagine what the right behavior, right words, or right attitude would be. Proceed to practice them during the week. (Use the "Examples of Righteous Fruit" list in the Appendix for ideas to spur your thinking.)

Also, continue your fast. Walk in repentance. *Stop* your wrong behavior and *go* in the right direction. Walk in the right behavior, right thinking, and right speaking, trusting in God.

Close in ACTS Prayer

Adoration - Praise God for Who He Is

Confession - Admit Your Sins with a Repentant Heart

Thanksgiving - Thank God for All He Has Done, Is Doing, and Is Going to Do

Supplication - Make Your Requests to God for Yourself and On Behalf of Others.

Notes

CHAPTER 8

A Fruitful Harvest: Ongoing Weeding and Planting—In the Power of the Spirit!

All of a sudden, out of nowhere it seemed, I was overcome with grief. I realized with a new level of clarity that I was never going to be without my flesh. The enemy, Satan, would tirelessly seek to employ the most effective methods at the most opportune times to attack. The world would continue to batter my hull. And my flesh would relentlessly seek to satisfy its own desires within and be prone to succumb to pressure from without.

As hard as I might try I knew I would never be able to strip myself of the flesh and be done with "her." As I was becoming more and more aware of the sweet and tender and beautiful Spirit of the Lord within me, I was deeply saddened that He is subject to residing within my hopeless frame. But I also knew that somehow, even when we don't understand, God is glorified in our weakness—that it's not about me, it is all about Him!

I cried out to the Lord in my grief, pleading with Him to please help me! I don't want people to have to deal with me. I long for them to see Jesus! I then called a dear friend. Her heart ached with compassion as she listened to my pain, but she was quick to say, "It is in that weakness, in that vulnerable vessel, that the power and holiness of God is much glorified!" Think of it … God in such an earthy vessel! The sooner we admit that there is nothing good within us apart from Christ, and confess that we are unable to overcome our flesh in our own strength, the faster we run to the cross and the quicker comes the rescue! Our flesh is put aside and Christ is exalted.

In the midst of the crucible of my human limitations, I prayed and felt the grace of God peel the blinders off my human understanding. He brought me to a point of dependence upon Christ. He reminded me of what Paul professed in 2 Corinthians 12:9: "But he said to me, 'My grace is sufficient for you, for my power is made perfect in weakness.'" In our humanness we can be so overwhelmed with our emotions, our passions, and our weakness! We see God's holiness and His standards, and we see our inability … we see ourselves fall so far short of the mark. We forget that God saw our weakness and our inability from the beginning and that He has given us Jesus Christ and His grace. Paul, like us, clearly sees his weakness but also clearly comprehends the power of Christ within him. He declares to the Corinthians, "Therefore I will boast all the more gladly of my weaknesses, so that the power of Christ may rest upon me" (2 Corinthians 12:20). He publically proclaims what he absolutely believes privately: Yes, I am a sinner! I am weak! I cannot do it!

We are sinners, we are weak, and we are prone to wander. But at the same time we are also saints! We are saints who have been given the Holy Spirit, Christ within. We are saints who have been given faith to walk in the Spirit. We have been given faith so that we have a means to access the grace and the power that has been given to us in Christ by the Holy Spirit. We have been given faith so that we can accomplish that which the Lord has purchased us to do: "For you were saved by grace through faith. And this is not your own doing; it is the gift of God, not a result of works, so that no one may boast. For we are his workmanship, created in Christ Jesus for good works, which God prepared beforehand, that we should walk in them" (Ephesians 2:8-10).

We must remember that we are not alone—for Christ lives within us! Christ—the one who created the heavens and the earth, Christ—the one who calmed the sea, Christ—the one who made the blind see and the deaf to hear and the lame to walk, Christ—the one who raised Lazarus from the tomb after having been dead four days, Christ—the one who lived, died, and rose again!

This Christ, *the* Christ, lives in you! The life that you now live in the flesh, you must live by faith in the Son of God who loved you and gave himself for you (Galatians 2:20)! Christ is our very righteousness! Paul calls us to be instruments of righteousness (Romans 6:13). We were born of the Spirit to bear fruit—His fruit!

What does that look like in our daily life? When you examine your tree illustration and see the roots of sin that lie below and the fruits that sin produces, ask yourself what is required of you to put off that sin, that unrighteousness, and put on righteousness. God's Word is clear. It gives us instruction on what to do and how to live like Christ, but it can't give us the power. We can replace a lie with the truth, but we cannot live that truth in our own strength, at least not for long. It wouldn't be faith. It wouldn't be grace! In order to live like Christ, we must believe it is only through Christ and by His Spirit who lives within us that we are able. And we must ask Him, believing He can and will do it, and walk out that life in faith.

So then, what do you do tomorrow when you face that wall of fear? When you want to eat and know that you shouldn't? When you feel the anger welling up and about to overflow? When you are so frustrated you want to scream? When you want to check out again and just sit in front of the TV instead of spending time with the Lord? What, or shall I say whom, will you choose? Will you choose to believe that the power you need to overcome resides within you? Will you choose Christ instead of yourself? Will you choose to glorify God and be an instrument of righteousness, or will you choose to dishonor Him and be an instrument of unrighteousness? It is not a matter of reasoning; it is a matter of resurrection. Christ lives within us, and it's by faith that He is lived out in our lives instead of ourselves. We choose Him by faith.

Remember Moses' parents. They could have chosen fear but they chose faith: "By faith Moses, when he was born, was hidden for three months by his parents, because they saw that the child was beautiful, and they were not afraid of the king's edict" (Hebrews 11:23). Remember Moses when he chose to follow God rather than stay where he was and indulge his flesh: "By faith Moses, when he was grown up, refused to be called the son of Pharaoh's daughter, choosing rather to be mistreated with the people of God than to enjoy the fleeting pleasures of sin. He considered the reproach of Christ greater wealth than the treasures of Egypt, for he was looking to the reward" (v. 24-26). Remember how Moses, who trusted in God and in His power to protect him and God's people, left Egypt with all of the Israelites: "By faith he left Egypt, not being afraid of the anger of the king, for he endured as seeing him who is invisible" (v. 27). Remember Joshua, who faced an insurmountable problem, and by faith followed God and His ways and not his own: "By faith the walls of Jericho fell down after they had been encircled for seven days" (v. 30). It is faith in God and in His power—not in their own ability, not in their own ways, and not in their own righteousness—that these men carried out God's plan for their lives. Without faith we cannot please God.

In that hour of need, when we are feeling overcome by our feelings or our circumstances, when you feel fear, anger, or pain, remember that it is no longer you who live but Christ who lives within you. Your flesh no longer has power to control you. It may feel like it does, but it's just an illusion. In the midst of that hour, all you may see is your fear, your anger, or your frustration; you may not be able to see Christ in you at all. You may not feel Christ in you at all. But faith is in the unseen! So believe in what you cannot "see" at that moment. Believe that Christ does dwell within you and tell yourself that the overwhelming feeling of fear, of anger, or of despair is merely a shadow of fear, an illusion. Tell yourself, "If I no longer live and Christ lives within me, I will choose to believe that He can overcome. I do not have to give into my feelings or my circumstances."

I will not identify or offer myself to unrighteousness but will instead choose Christ and identify with Christ and offer myself to be an instrument of righteousness. I do not have to fear—I can have faith and trust in God.

So as you are aware of your limitations, your circumstances, your feelings, your passions, choose to believe that God has given you everything you need; choose to believe He has given us himself. Your weakness? God's strength. Your sin? God's grace. Your enemy? God's shield and strong tower of protection. Your fear? God's faithfulness. Your temptation? God's deliverance. You have heard the expression, "You get out of life what you put into it." Or maybe you are familiar with the Scripture, "Whoever sows sparingly will also reap sparingly, and whoever sows bountifully will also reap bountifully" (2 Corinthians 9:6). We are

God's field, ripe for harvest. What we really believe and how we act on that belief will make all the difference in the harvest from our lives.

Believing who you are in Christ, believing who Christ is, and fully apprehending what you have been given in Christ will be the difference between feast or famine, the difference between a bountiful eternal harvest (here on earth and in heaven) or just merely gathering scraps under the table. The Lord wants to give us a passion for His vision. He wants to give us eyes to see the fields ripe for harvest! So often we look at things as they are and have a hard time seeing them as they could be and really believing that we can make a difference. The harvest begins with us.

I remember when we first saw the property where we currently live. The minute we stepped on the property we sensed that it could be a special and nurturing place for our family. There was a small Beatrix Potter garden in the backyard, complete with gates and arches at both ends and fully fenced in. Once upon a time you could tell that it had been picturesque, well kept, right out of the pages of Peter Rabbit. But when we found it, it was completely overgrown with weeds as tall as the fence. And within a couple years the weeds were 6-feet tall. Well, I had a vision. I thought we could begin small ... clear the weeds and plant a few tomatoes. I thought next year we could add more.

Well, that is exactly what we did. I say we, but I really mean my husband. He cleared the land and planted six tomato plants, and we yielded a huge harvest of thirty to forty tomatoes! Clearly we are not blessed with green thumbs. Our friend planted 62 tomato plants. Last time I talked with her, their yield was five thousand tomatoes—and counting! Our output was less than one percent of hers! You will reap what you sow. I am a city girl—not a farmer ... and no real vision or heart to be one. Paula, our friend, is a farmer's daughter, and she had knowledge, belief, and vision. She knew what that plot of land would produce with the right amount of care, fertilizer, water, and sun. What we do with what we've been given is definitely dependent upon what we really believe and what we do with what we believe.

Our harvest is multiplied when we understand and truly believe who we are, who Christ is, and what God has given to us in Christ. And it is utterly, absolutely, exclusively dependent upon it. We may merely be jars of clay, but we have been given much! We are filled with the Holy Spirit. Jesus instructs His disciples during His last days with them before He ascends to heaven, "Truly, truly, I say to you, whoever believes in me will also do the works that I do; and greater works than these will he do, because I am going to the Father. Whatever you ask in my name, this I will do, that the Father may be glorified in the Son. If you ask me anything in my name, I will do it" (John 14:12-14). Some of us have been Christians, very committed Christians, for years and even decades. Our parents may even have been Christians.

Is it possible that those of us who have known Him and seen His power in our lives have seen enough change and fruit that we think, "Well, we reaped a fair harvest of tomatoes—that was a good harvest." But I believe He wants to do more, much, much more. Others of you have been Christians and haven't seen much fruit, to the point that you think maybe you've been given a rotten plot of land and that it is never going to produce. But He wants all of us to have faith—much faith—not in who we are but in who He is and what He has given to us. He desires for us to have a faith that is pregnant with great expectation; a faith that apprehends the power and glory of God; a faith that wants to know Jesus and follow Him in radical obedience, putting to death the flesh, the old woman, and believing that all things are possible through Him: "And without faith it is impossible to please him, for whoever would draw near to God must believe that he exists and that he rewards those who seek him" (Hebrews 11:6). I am challenged by this call. Initially, I will step out to follow Him, but the further I follow Him, the further I am from the crowd. It is lonely out there, and I become unsure! I am following God not knowing where I am going! Faith equals fruit; much faith equals much fruit. Believe God, believe His Word, and obey His Word by faith … that equals a Fruitful Harvest!

So here is the question: Will you choose faith? What do you want to spring forth from your heart? What type of fruit do you want growing from your life and your decisions? What fruit do you want to be displayed before your friends and your family? What kind of harvest do you want to reap? If you sow righteousness, you will reap righteousness. "Sow for yourselves righteousness; reap steadfast love; break up your fallow ground, for it is the time to seek the LORD, that he may come and rain righteousness upon you" (Hosea 10:12). May the Lord rain righteousness upon you! By faith, sow righteousness, and may you reap a full, abundant, fruit-filled harvest!

Interacting with God and His Word

Read the passage below and ponder the blessings that God has for you when you choose to believe as Abraham believed. Remember to write your thoughts or answers in a prayer journal or in the space provided at the end of the chapter.

Galatians 3:6-9

Just as Abraham "believed God, and it was counted to him as righteousness"? 7 Know then that it is those of faith who are the sons of Abraham. 8 And the Scripture, foreseeing that God would justify the Gentiles by faith, preached the gospel beforehand to Abraham, saying, "In you shall all the nations be blessed." 9 So then, those who are of faith are blessed along with Abraham, the man of faith.

If we are Christians, two very different principles of power dwell within us—the flesh and the Spirit. The flesh is against the Spirit. We cannot please God when we are acting in the flesh. Remember clearly that you have a choice—to sow the deeds of the Spirit or the deeds of the flesh. Read Galatians 5:16-17, 19-21.

Galatians 5:16-17, 19-21

But I say, walk by the Spirit, and you will not gratify the desires of the flesh. 17 For the desires of the flesh are against the Spirit, and the desires of the Spirit are against the flesh, for these are opposed to each other, to keep you from doing the things you want to do ... 19 Now the works of the flesh are evident: sexual immorality, impurity, sensuality, 20 idolatry, sorcery, enmity, strife, jealousy, fits of anger, rivalries, dissensions, divisions, 21 envy, drunkenness, orgies, and things like these. I warn you, as I warned you before, that those who do such things will not inherit the kingdom of God.

Where do you see your struggle most clearly with the flesh? What is keeping you from completely submitting to the Spirit, to Christ? What is it that you don't want to lose? Now read Galatians 5:22-24.

Galatians 5:22-24

But the fruit of the Spirit is love, joy, peace, patience, kindness, goodness, faithfulness, 23 gentleness, self-control; against such things there is no law. 24 And those who belong to Christ Jesus have crucified the flesh with its passions and desires.

You have been given all of this and more in Christ. In every step we take, each thought we think, and every word we say, we have a choice to walk in the flesh and serve the flesh or to walk in the Spirit and serve Christ. Will you believe that God has truly given you all of the righteousness you need to walk in righteousness? Will you act on that belief? Joyfully anticipate victory as you exercise your faith and choose to root out your sin.

In closing, take a moment to write a prayer to the Lord asking Him to give you the desire, the grace, and the wisdom to walk in the Spirit.

Search My Heart, O God

Prayerfully read the following excerpts from Psalm 139.

Psalm 139

1   O LORD, you have searched me and known me!
2   You know when I sit down and when I rise up;
        you discern my thoughts from afar.
3   You search out my path and my lying down
        and are acquainted with all my ways.
4   Even before a word is on my tongue,
        behold, O LORD, you know it altogether.
5   You hem me in, behind and before,
        and lay your hand upon me.

6   Such knowledge is too wonderful for me;
        it is high; I cannot attain it.

7   Where shall I go from your Spirit?
        Or where shall I flee from your presence?

8   If I ascend to heaven, you are there!
        If I make my bed in Sheol, you are there!

9   If I take the wings of the morning
        and dwell in the uttermost parts of the sea,

10 even there your hand shall lead me,
        and your right hand shall hold me.

11 If I say, "Surely the darkness shall cover me,
        and the light about me be night,"

12 even the darkness is not dark to you;
        the night is bright as the day,
        for darkness is as light with you.

13 For you formed my inward parts;
        you knitted me together in my mother's womb.

14 I praise you, for I am fearfully and wonderfully made.
        Wonderful are your works;
        my soul knows it very well.

15 My frame was not hidden from you,
        when I was being made in secret,
        intricately woven in the depths of the earth.

16 Your eyes saw my unformed substance;
        in your book were written, every one of them,
        the days that were formed for me,
        when as yet there was none of them.

17 How precious to me are your thoughts, O God!
        How vast is the sum of them!

18 If I would count them, they are more than the sand.
        I awake, and I am still with you.

23 Search me, O God, and know my heart!
        Try me and know my thoughts!

24 And see if there be any grievous way in me,
    and lead me in the way everlasting!

Humbly and vulnerably go before the Lord today as you have throughout this study and ask Him to search your heart. Know that there is no reason to fear. He loves you dearly right where you are and is delighted in your perseverance! He is your tender shepherd who will lead you in the paths of righteousness for His name's sake.

I encourage you as your read your Bible to continue to look for Scriptures that will lead you to replace your roots of sin with roots of righteousness. Ask the Lord to show you the way and He will do it. And continue your fast if the Lord has led you to do so. By faith, walk in repentance and in righteousness, trusting in Christ and His power and His righteousness! He will be glorified!

Close in ACTS Prayer

Adoration - Praise God for Who He Is

Confession - Admit Your Sins with a Repentant Heart

Thanksgiving - Thank God for All He Has Done, Is Doing, and Is Going to Do

Supplication - Make Your Requests to God for Yourself and On Behalf of Others.

Notes

Notes

Appendix

The Pride Tree

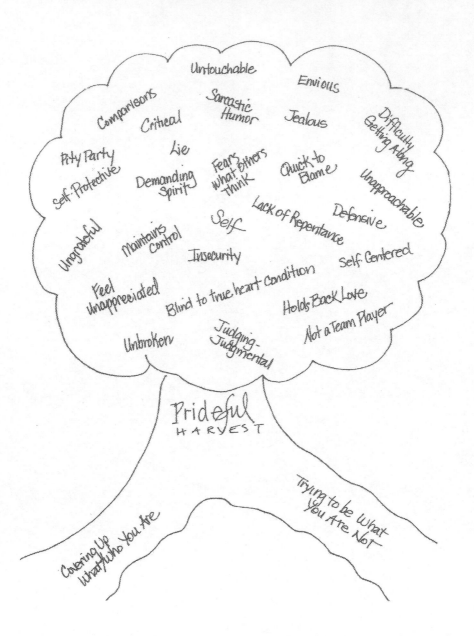

Untouchable

Envious

Comparisons   Critical   Sarcastic   Jealous   Difficulty
                           Humor   Getting Along

Pity Party   Lie   Fears   Quick to   Unapproachable
Self Protective Demanding what Others Blame
                   Spirit   Think   Defensive

Ungrateful   Self   Lack of Repentance
         Maintains
          Control   Insecurity   Self Centered
Feel
Unappreciated   Blind to true heart Condition   Holds Back Love

                  Judging-   Not a Team Player
Unbroken   Judgmental

Prideful
H A R V E S T

Trying to be What
You Are Not

Covering Up
What/Who You Are

86

Examples of Sinful Fruit

Irritated tone with family or with others
Interrupting/not letting another speak
Thinking less of others
Unwillingness to listen
Not being caring to sales clerks
Procrastinating
Speeding
Hiding money or things from spouse
Rushing around
Sleeping too much/being lazy
Critical comments
Giving "The Look"
Picking on others' weaknesses or idiosyncrasies
Grabbing or physically harsh/abrupt
Unkind, harsh words
Wasting time
Slamming doors
Sighing or huffing as a response
Rolling eyes
Defensive or argumentative
Snide remarks
Pouting
Comments under breath
Fudging the truth/Embellishing/Lying
Holding a grudge
Withholding love
Fearfully not being oneself
Not doing Quiet Time
Afraid/Ashamed to share faith and truth
Watching too much TV
Eating too much
Not picking up after self

Too much time on phone or computer
Friends more important than family
Shopping when shouldn't be
Agenda-focused, not Christ-focused
Inattentive or checked out
Worrying about what others think
Projecting what others are thinking
Worrying about money/circumstances
Not following through on commitments
Perpetually being late

Ask Yourself

Have you lied about something?

Have you purposefully withheld information from someone?

Have you spoken unkindly about someone?

Have you used words that would not glorify God?

Have you embellished a story just a "tiny bit" to make it more exciting or more about you?

Are you more concerned about being right than about being Godly?

Are you ignoring someone because you are mad at them?

Have you thought unkind thoughts about someone?

Have you judged the purchases of someone else?

Have you judged the way someone else is spending his or her time?

Have you judged someone else's decision?

Have you compared your husband to someone else's husband?

Have you tried to manipulate others?

Have you been disrespectful to your husband or to anyone in any way?

Have you used a harsh tone with your husband or with your children?

Are you trying to be someone's Holy Spirit?

Have you disciplined in anger?

Have you been spending too much time watching TV?

Have you been spending too much time shopping?

Have you been spending too much time decorating your house?

Have you been spending too much time on the phone?

Are you tithing a tenth of your income or an amount considered sacrificial?

Are you spending too much money on unimportant things?

Are you doing something that is not God's will but it is solely to impress others?

Are you considering others before yourself?

Is there anything in your life that God has told you to do that you are dragging your feet on?

Are you spending too much time/energy/money on your outward appearance?

Is the motive behind the way you spend your time about impressing others?

Are you resentful towards someone because of something he or she did or said?

Have you purposefully excluded someone from something?

Have you spoken out of anger to someone?

Have you talked about someone behind his or her back?

Are you making the time to do your quiet time?

Have you spoken to someone about something that God clearly wants you to speak up about?

Do you need to ask someone to forgive you for something?

Are you spending enough time with your children?

Are your priorities in order?

Have you compared your children with other children, wishing that your children were more like them?

Have you secretly been happy about something that went wrong in someone else's life?

Are you a "doer"—doing or buying lots of things for other people?

Are you doing these things so that the spotlight is on you or on God?

Have you told someone you would pray for her or him and then didn't?

Have you bragged about some area of your life to anyone?

Is there someone or something that you are making an idol out of?

Do you expect too much out of others?

Is there something you are doing in your own flesh and strength rather than relying on God?

Are you making the most of your time during the day?

Are you doing your responsibilities around the house with excellence and in a timely manner?

Are you working for God or for man?

Unrighteous Vs. Righteous Roots

Use this list to help determine your roots, what lies underneath and leads to the fruit displayed in your life.

Unrighteous	Righteous
Selfish and Self-seeking	Others Oriented
Dishonest	Honest
Frightened	Courageous
Inconsiderate	Considerate
Prideful	Humble
Greedy	Generous
Lustful	Chaste or Pure
Angry	Calm
Envious	Grateful
Slothful or Lazy	Active
Gluttonous	Moderate
Impatient	Patient
Intolerant	Merciful
Resentful	Forgiving
Hateful	Loving
Doing Harmful Acts	Doing Good Deeds
Exhibiting Self-pity	Being Self-forgetful
Exhibiting Self-justification	Seeking God's Will
Self-important	Modest
Self-condemning	Receiver of Mercy
Suspicious	Trusting
Doubtful	Faithful

Examples of Righteous Fruit

Sending a note of encouragement
Praying for others regularly
Stopping by to say Hi or dropping a line
Listening attentively
Loving heart and tone w/family and others
Thinking of others
Engaging in conversation and encourage sales clerks
Speaking the truth in love
Following the Lord, not knowing where you're going
Inspiring others
Taking time to spiritually train your children
Taking one step at a time
Keeping your word
Making encouraging comments
Love, love, love
Being completely honest
Being transparent
Being vulnerable
Being ready and willing to serve
Expressing/demonstrating love
Being yourself with confidence
Making quiet time with the Lord a priority
Making the most of every minute
Making time for friends
Using moderation in TV and movie watching
Entertainment in moderation
Upholding rules in a loving and consistent manner
Enjoying others
Holding children accountable in a loving, firm manner
Being flexible
Eating when hungry, eating healthy
Christ above all, then family

Scripture memorization and meditation
Loving others where they are
Enjoying the Lord and His word
Conforming to the Lord
Spending time with your children
Obeying the Lord
Following through on a commitment
Diligently completing a task
Persevering through something difficult
Letting go of your agenda
Doing what your husband asks of you
Using gentle manner/tone/words
Handling a situation the way the Lord wants
Responding with patience
Trusting the Lord when you've been misunderstood

The Humility Tree

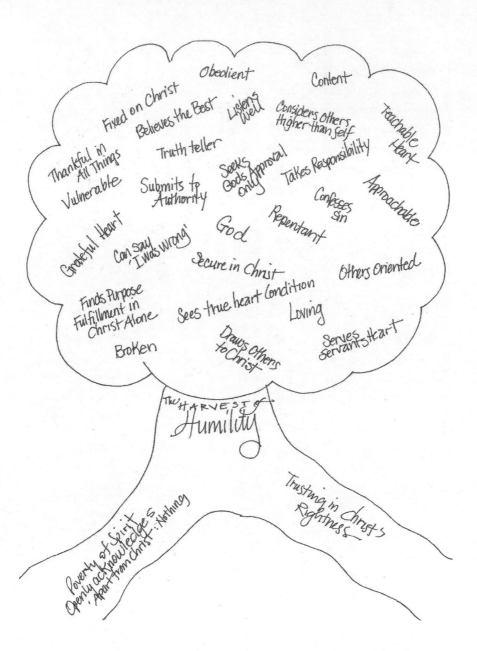

The Gospel of Our Salvation
by Scott Kaczorowski

The Bible teaches that we are all separated from God because of sin (Eph. 2:1-4, 12). We are spiritually dead inside. And we don't have to do anything for this to be true of us. Because of Adam's sin, we are simply born that way (Ps. 51:5). We are spiritual stillbirths. If we remain in this condition until the day of our physical death, this spiritual separation from God will be permanent, eternal separation from Him in hell (Rev. 20:11-15; 21:8). This is a terrifying prospect if we have really contemplated it. We need salvation!

God sent His Son, Jesus Christ, to rescue us from this fate worse than (physical) death. Jesus died on the cross, taking the death that we should have died because of our sin: "He himself bore our sins in his body on the tree ..." (1 Pet. 2:24). This provides a way of salvation.

If we would be saved, we must place our faith in Christ (John 3:16-18; Rom. 3:22-25). Faith is believing in our hearts that Jesus is the Son of God, that He died on the cross for our sins, that He was raised to life three days later, and that He is Lord over all things and entrusting ourselves to Him (cf. Rom. 10:9-13).

Left to ourselves, we would never place our faith in Jesus. Sin has blinded our minds and hearts so much that even if we intellectually believed all of this about Jesus and knew that salvation could be found in no other way, we still would choose to turn our backs on God. So God graciously steps in. Before he created the world, He knew that sin would enter it and that it would render those under its power unable even to turn in faith to Him (John 6:44a). So out of His grace, God decided that He would rescue some from this plight. The Bible refers to this as predestination or election (Eph. 1:3-6). To those whom God has chosen, He gives saving faith (Eph. 2:8-9; Phil. 1:29; 1 Tim. 1:14) and true repentance (Acts 11:18; 2 Tim. 2:25) and effectively causes them to come to Jesus (John 6:37, 44).

When people place their faith in Christ, they are saved. On the one hand they are justified—God declares that they are completely righteous in His sight (Rom. 3:24). All their sins are forgiven. They also become God's children. The Bible refers to this as adoption (Rom. 8:15-17; Eph. 1:5). God also sends His Holy Spirit to live inside of them—they are indwelt (Rom. 8:9-11; Gal. 4:6) and sealed by the Spirit of God (Eph. 1:13-14). The Holy Spirit also baptizes them, incorporating them into the body of Christ (1 Cor. 12:13) and gives them spiritual gifts so that they can serve the body of Christ (1 Cor. 12:4-11). Every believer in Jesus has been baptized by the Holy Spirit and has spiritual gifts. *Any* spiritual gift is the result of the baptism of the Holy Spirit.

Those who place their faith in Christ have been born again (John 1:12-13; 1 John 5:1). They are new creations: "Therefore, if anyone is in Christ, he is a new creation. The old has passed away; behold the new has come" (2 Cor. 5:17). As such, although sin still lives in them, it no longer has power over them. They are not to obey sin but Jesus Christ (Rom. 6:1-4, 16-19).

But the overcoming of sin in the life of a believer does not happen in an instant. It is a slow process of growth in holiness throughout their lives as they become more and more like Jesus. It will not be until we are in the presence of the Lord in heaven (or until the Lord returns) that sin will be completely done. But the believer today is to continue to press forward in holiness by putting their remaining sin to death, relying on the power that the Holy Spirit supplies: " … put off your old self, which belongs to your former manner of life and is corrupt through deceitful desires, and to be renewed in the spirit of your minds, and to put on the new self, created after the likeness of God in true righteousness and holiness" (Eph. 4:22-24).

As we have seen, salvation is experienced in stages so to speak. There are aspects of it that we have the moment we believe in Jesus (i.e. complete forgiveness of sins, the indwelling of the Holy Spirit). There are other aspects of it that we grow into over time, such as closer communion with God and more and more victory over sin in our lives. And there are components of it that are equally part of our salvation, but we will not experience until we die (such as perfect sinlessness) or Christ returns (our transformed resurrection body). So the language that is sometimes used for this is appropriate: "We *are* saved. We *are being* saved. We *will be* saved."

When salvation is complete and we stand as eternal examples of God's grace (Eph. 1:6, 11; Eph. 2:6-7), then the goodness of God in rescuing us from the awfulness of our predicament will shine forever and ever. In salvation, we receive all the benefit. But God gets all the glory.

> "To him who sits on the throne and to the Lamb be blessing
> and honor and glory and might forever and ever!"
> (Rev. 5:13)

Works Cited

Foster, Richard. *Celebration of Discipline*. New York: Harper and Row Publishers, 1978.

Lloyd-Jones, D. Martin. *Studies in the Sermon on the Mount*, Vol. II. Grand Rapids, MI: William B. Eerdmans Publishing Company, 1959-60.

Murray, Andrew. *With Christ in the School of Prayer.* Springdale, PA: Whitaker House, 1981.

Owen, John. *Of the Mortification of Sin in Believers*, Chapter 2, no. 6. Edinburgh: Banner of Truth Trust, 1967.

Spurgeon, Charles H. Ed. Alistair Begg. *Morning and Evening*. Wheaton, IL: Crossway, 2003.

Endnotes

[1] John Owen, *Of the Mortification of Sin in Believers*, Chapter 2, no. 6 (Edinburgh: Banner of Truth Trust, 1967). *Original quote modified for women.

[2] Same Hebrew word used in Deut. 6:4 to mean an understanding heart, an idiom for a hearing and obedient heart.

[3] Charles H. Spurgeon, edited by Alistair Begg, *Morning and Evening* (Wheaton, IL: Crossway, 2003), entry for May 21, Evening.

[4] Andrew Murray, *With Christ in the School of Prayer* (Springdale, PA: Whitaker House, 1981), pp 100-101.

[5] Richard Foster, *Celebration of Discipline* (New York: Harper and Row Publishers, 1978), pp 41-42.

[6] D. Martin Lloyd-Jones, *Studies in the Sermon on the Mount*, Vol. II (William B. Eerdmans Publishing Company, 1959-60), p 38.

Printed in the United States
By Bookmasters